Homage to the Tragic Muse

ANGELOS TERZAKIS

HOMAGE
TO THE
TRAGIC
MUSE

TRANSLATED FROM THE GREEK BY

ATHAN H. ANAGNOSTOPOULOS

WITH A FOREWORD BY CEDRIC H. WHITMAN

HOUGHTON MIFFLIN COMPANY   BOSTON 1978

*Adapted from Library of Congress Cataloging
in Publication Data*
Terzakis, Angelos Dēmētriou, date
  Homage to the tragic muse.

  Translation of Aphierōma stēn tragikē mousa.
  1. Tragedy.   I. Title.
PN1892.T4713   808.2'51   78-15045
ISBN 0-395-27088-X

Printed in the United States of America

S 10 9 8 7 6 5 4 3 2 1

Foreword

TRAGEDY, since the Greeks invented it, has taken so
many shapes and embraced so many kinds of meaning
that it now seems as hopeless for the literary critic to arrive
at a single definition as it is for the philologist to determine
the original significance of the very word. But if the meaning of tragedy seems as elusive as the meaning of life itself,
it has seldom been seriously doubted, as it has been with
life, that tragedy has meaning; and that is the real reason
for its existence. Out of a series of given events, apparently
as pointless as they are shattering to contemplate, the art
of the tragic poet creates a coherence that, it must always
be remembered, is not a philosophic key to the ultimate
mystery, but rather an invention, a structure wrought from
the internal tensions of poetic utterance; and in that structure is an affirmation, a reassurance whose substance, however, cannot quite be precisely fixed or grasped. That
tragedy, for all its world of suffering, has a positive dimension is a commonplace, but to define that dimension in
any systematic universal terms is quite another matter.
All that emerges, all that might be commonly agreed to

emerge, is an enlargement of belief, a reappraisal of the human spirit through action and language, leading to a moral vision too inclusive, in its breadth, depth, and elevation, to be encompassed, so far, by even the best-laid theory of tragedy. The art seems often better served by those critics who can search and articulate their own responses to the tragic experience, in its various forms, alert to all the constituent subtleties of conception and speech that make each drama work.

In *Homage to the Tragic Muse,* Angelos Terzakis, one of Greece's most distinguished men of letters — dramatist, essayist, and in essence a poet — has gathered the thinking of a lifetime about tragedy, as a phenomenon of the theater, as a poetic structure with its own inherent verity, and as an assessment of man against what may or may not be properly called the cosmos. It is a frankly subjective book containing, as his Prologue says, all the things he did not say to his students during his years of teaching drama, because he did not deem it his right to "take young minds by surprise." Yet it is really written for the young, people with "fresh soul, unblemished conscience, incorruptible sensibility"; for, as the last chapter explains, youth is the Tragic Age. The book's subjectivity should not be mistaken for self-indulgence, though its manner is wayward, impulsive, and sometimes even imperious. This is no collection of impressionistic observations, however sensitive. It is a passionate examination of the author's own understanding of tragedy as seen through several tragedies, an argument pursued more rigorously than may at first appear, constantly being restated and newly qualified, and emerging on page after page in formulations sometimes lyrical, sometimes braced by the wiry elegance of epigram. It is a book already famous in Greece, and now available

in an English translation that is a manifest labor of love
by the scholar who is also giving us English versions of
Seferis' journals.

This kind of essay is not without its precedents. It belongs, in fact, in the illustrious tradition of Kierkegaard,
Nietzsche, and Heidegger, whose writings on tragedy, by-
products of their larger work, have adumbrated some of
its greater truths. Confessedly Existentialist, though hap-
pily not marred by the characteristic jargon, this study
follows worthily in the wake of those who first looked
behind the façade of Idealist philosophy into the turbulent
fertility of the Greek mind of the fifth century B.C. Moreover, its author has one advantage over his great forerun-
ners: Terzakis is a Greek and, as he says, "The world of
tragedy is the Greek world." No Christian presuppositions
haunt these pages; for though Greece is a Christian country, it often seems easier for a Greek today to set aside his
Christianity and reach backward toward antiquity with a
hand unmediated by the intervening cultures. Nor is there
either history of tragedy or theory of tragedy to limit or
distort the critic's range of response to what he finds immediately before him in the texts he reads and imagines
in the theater. Instead, the book is a kind of symptomatic
analysis, and synthesis, of the various inner forces, aesthetic and moral, that make for tragedy, as realized in
selected works of Sophocles, Marlowe, and Shakespeare
primarily, with less extensive treatment of Aeschylus,
Euripides, Racine, and a number of moderns. Given the
openness of approach, the receptiveness to each new structure, and the absence of any a priori formula of interpretation, it is remarkable how plays found in widely separated periods concur in being recognizable as tragedies,
though no one seems to be archetypal, while others ap-

proach that status but fall, in his view, short. Much of Terzakis' criterion for tragedy depends on the central figure, the tragic hero, but there is much else besides.

For the book, however kaleidoscopic, does have a central theme. The theme is the tragic ethos itself, which Terzakis says is framed from a "cosmological standpoint." Tragedy arises from "an antithetical relationship between our conscience and the world, the point where they chafe and produce a spark"; and it is this "ontological antinomy," this "affirmed antithesis of man with the world order," that keeps reappearing in various guises throughout the analyses of such disparate works as *Oedipus Tyrannus, Dr. Faustus, Julius Caesar, Hippolytus, Romeo and Juliet,* and *Antony and Cleopatra,* to mention only the principal ones. If much in the analysis depends on the tragic hero, it is one of the book's great virtues that it keeps constantly before us that tragic heroes are not actual persons — that disastrous hypostasis which still infects so much tragic criticism — but that they and their actions are one and inseparable. The tragic hero is that "which does not exist without being crushed"; tragic heroes only "exist to give cosmological meaning to the cause they serve." All is a construction by the poet, who arranges and disposes as his sense of the tragic ethos guides him. The theory of Fate as tragic cause is refreshingly dismissed as "the facile alibi of intellectual complacency," and the theory of tragic flaw finds no place. Instead, "Tragedy is the drama of metaphysical freedom."

It would be lengthy to go on about Terzakis' revealing words on the nature of Apollo in *Oedipus,* or the relation of the Sphinx to the oracles in that play; or *Faustus* as the "tragedy of God's silence"; or the fundamentally tragic character of eros itself in the tragedies of love; indeed, the chapter on *Romeo and Juliet* is in many ways the best. But summary and quotation cannot convey the compelling truthfulness of the book. It is not an easy book; it requires sustained intellective effort. Intensely personal and intimate in tone throughout, it is heady stuff. It is also an odd book in certain ways, going at its own pace and feeling no need for strictly balanced treatment of the various texts, provided that what is needful is said of each. It is a quest after the spirit of tragedy, and it leads wherever tragedy's uncompromisingly ontological nature can best be discerned. The reader is in the hands of a safe guide, a critic whose scholarship is driven by an intuition of surest touch; it is as if a Greek poet had come to claim his rightful inheritance, and in the process to help the English-speaking world to a clearer disposition toward its own.

Cedric H. Whitman

Contents

Homage to the Tragic Muse

Prologue

THIS BOOK, which as primary source material has occupied me nearly as long as the work of a lifetime,
started out without plan or clear aim. For many years,
while studying the theater or writing plays, as well as
during my lectures on dramatic theory in the Drama
School of the Greek National Theater, and especially at
the end of a lecture, when I stepped out of the classroom,
I used to jot down notes. Sometimes I kept them, sometimes I lost them. Needless to say, the ones that are lost
seem the best today — mainly because they are lost. Often, I meant to gather those that were left, put them in
order, and compose a whole with some coherence. I kept
postponing it. I felt that I had not yet recorded what was
stirring within me and what the question of tragedy demanded of me.

Finally, at a certain moment, I realized that this wandering would end only with my life. Then I found a solution
out of necessity: Instead of sitting down and writing a
systematic work, something that for one reason or another
does not suit me, a treatise on tragedy, let's say, I decided

to express my various thoughts about tragedy. This solved
many problems for me at once: First, it did not compel me
to exhaust the inexhaustible. Second, it did not tempt
me to try to express the inconceivable. Third, it rescued
me from the danger of appearing dogmatic, of speaking
ex cathedra. Fourth, it allowed me to give my text a subjective tone. This last, I confess, lured me more than all
the others. The reason for this I hope will become clear
by itself.

It is self-evident that only a small part of the material
that I have been gathering for many years now has entered
here, as was true in my lectures, too. Here, because a book
is not a mere concoction; in my lectures, on the other
hand, because one does not speak to young people about
such matters. Not that they are not mature enough to
understand; on the contrary, only young people have the
necessary receptiveness. Whenever I have tried to communicate on this level with men already formed, I have
failed lamentably. Mature for such speculations and full
knowledge is he who has a fresh soul, unblemished conscience, incorruptible sensibility. If, therefore, I have not
used the material I have mentioned in my lectures, it is
because their orientation was different, technical. And
because I did not consider it my right to take young minds
by surprise.

I do not conceal that I felt a shudder each time that,
either carried away by an analysis of a play or trying to
answer a crucial question, I involuntarily strayed into terri-
tories similar to those in this book. The soul of tragedy is
somber, its glance is fathomless. I have often seen — and
I have not forgotten — the startled eyes of young people
when some such allusions escaped from me. I then realized that with a clumsy gesture I had unveiled an edge of

the Holy Chalice. I hastened to cover it again, even with
an impertinent digression or an untimely joke.

I must add that anything cast into words, and most
especially written words, loses all its aura, that mist which
at moments brings to the surface exhalations from the
depths. Tragedy is a mystery that takes place down there.
This, I think, very few have understood, although they
say they have. Evidence of this is that men wise in other
ways ascribe the title of tragedy to the most irrelevant
texts, dramatic or narrative, as if it were a commendation,
an honorable distinction, a decoration one pins on whom-
ever one wants to please. Those of us who believe the
contrary know how pale and unfaithful words are, how
impotent to express the weight, the fervor, the authority,
the vibration that warns us of uttermost speculation. In
what I will try to say here, then, I will imply rather than
state. Analysis in art explains nothing; at its best it inter-
prets. And yet . . .

I would think very carefully before putting a bibliog-
raphy at the end of my text; it would give an appearance
of erudition where no pretense of wisdom is intended. I
detest utilitarian things, I am not at all a professor. Out
there I am (I always say this to my students) but an artist,
who has the madness of breaking into a monologue about
what he loves passionately. Indeed, why did Descartes
say that one exists because one thinks? I will dare to
argue and say: *Amo ergo sum.* I feel that I exist when I
love.

I

The Tragic Spirit

Aʙᴏᴠᴇ ᴀɴᴅ ʙᴇʏᴏɴᴅ tragedy as a genre of dramatic theater there exists an evocative yet undefined concept: the tragic spirit. What do we call tragic spirit? I hasten to state that my purpose is not to define its broader aspect, which transcends the theatrical realm and occasionally applies to actual persons, spiritual figures like Pascal, Kierkegaard, Nietzsche, or Dostoevski. We shall deal here purely with the stage space, because that is where the tragic spirit attains an affirmation so intense that, instead of restricting and confining itself, it on the contrary miraculously expands. We shall meet the improper usage of the concept "tragic" in the sphere of life, not of the stage.

But first one remark: beyond all manifestations of the tragic there exists something that appears to emerge as the ethos of Tragedy. If in drama — psychological or social drama — one discerns at once the concept "dramatic," if in comedy the element of the comic is self-evident, in tragedy the tragic is far more than a defining mark. Tragedy transcends the corresponding dramatic genre. Tragedy is a definite world view, a special way of seeing and evaluating the world. Through tragedy we have a special cosmological standpoint, an optical angle from which one can with candor and exultation observe oneself in the universe. It is for this reason that we speak of a "tragic ethos," whereas it is not possible to speak of a comic or dramatic ethos. Let us consider this distinction, latent in every evocation of the tragic, our first given. It will help us proceed.

When I speak about the tragic spirit I have in mind two assumptions: first that something uniform imbues the tragic genre, independent of its known varieties, and second that from the tragic genre emerges a definite conception of life. These two assumptions are one, in essence. This is not accidental nor should we consider it an illusion, as when we find something where we had already put it. In the distinctive nature of tragedy and in the tragic concept of life is hidden the seed of its origin: the existential concept of being. Through tragedy we descend to the roots of our anguished association with the world, of our conscious as well as inevitable involvement in its turmoil. Tragedy, in this sense, is an antithetical relationship between our conscience and the world, the point where they chafe and produce a spark.

The world, then, is not conceived as a framework. The world is the first and ultimate given, the reality that not only contains us but also expresses us. It is from here, from this threshold that the wandering begins. In order to set foot on firmer ground, I propose the following method: to look at five or six tragic heroes from the ancient theater and ask whether they have some common characteristic, a trait that refers not to their personalities but to the reality they express. I propose the ancient theater so that we will be dealing with the origin, with the first conception of the tragic. And I say heroes, not plays, because in a play it is natural for the tragic spirit to be refracted. The play is a correlation of relationships, situations, developments, whereas in the hero the tragic is embodied, blended, and definitive. In the hero as personality, individuality, and also as the bearer of a destiny. I admit that the method I propose may be considered arbitrary or prejudiced: "Why these heroes and not others?" I will begin my exploration, then, from this point.

I choose the heroes I have mentioned with one clear criterion: their developed initiative. I will not examine here whether it suits the tragic hero's nature to lack a keen initiative with regard to his circumstances; or what degree of free choice is necessary to guarantee the concept of responsibility, the susceptibility to retribution. By general consent, we accept that free will, active participation, and intellectual wholeness are necessary presuppositions, independent of the specific circumstances surrounding the hero. Our work will be facilitated if we choose heroes with unquestionably developed wills. I propose therefore: Prometheus and Eteocles from Aeschylus; from Sophocles, Oedipus and Antigone; from Euripides, Medea. I do not say that these five constitute an exception. I say that in these five the alien elements — supernatural intervention, derangement of mind, immutable destiny — are of secondary importance. This is fundamental, for it prohibits anything else from clouding the issue.

If in Orestes the question appears somewhat complex, not to say muddled, if in fact it is hard to discern what in the end drives Agamemnon's son — voluntary conformity with moral duty or Apollo's exhortation — in the case of Prometheus I have no doubts. A figure belonging to a

superhuman race of beings quarreled with Zeus, a new
and rebel god, and was defeated. But his defeat is implicit
in the rules of the game; it is its organic consequence.
Essentially, we are in a family circle: Titans against gods.
I now ask this question: If Prometheus had done what he
did, not for the sake of the human race but for a race of
beings kindred to him, would perhaps our involvement, an
element so fundamental to the "familiar" pleasure of tragedy, function as it does now? Of course the suffering of
the hero would remain, a feature that brings him nearly
to the human level. But we should not forget that in the
case of a later suffering prophet, Christ, He is not only the
Son of Joseph and Mary, the Son of Man, who moves us;
He is also the bearer of the sins of the world. In our
empathy, this first seed of tragic pity, is hidden an unconsciously selfish element, which is expiated because it
projects the self-love not of the individual but of the human race. Let us call *this* trait "humane."

I go on to Eteocles. The plane here is clearly human, the
circle of self-sacrifice confined: the city, the fatherland.
Instead of a prophet we have here a king who loves his
country. In addition, something dark looms in the distant
background, commingling its shadow with the radiance
of freedom. The ancestral *hamartia* (error, flaw) of the
Labdakids seems to blunt, to some extent, the free choice
of the king of Thebes. We wonder: Could it have hap
pened otherwise? Could Oedipus' son have escaped from
the cursed circle of his family? However, if we are more
careful, we will notice that the element of predestination
does not lessen Eteocles' grandeur; on the contrary, it
elevates it. It is precisely this which makes us feel that the
existence of a flaw, instead of exposing the hero's tragic
quality to doubt, underscores it. The conflict with the

higher order of things, which also constitutes the knot of the tragic, is not an arbitrary choice, the whim of an eccentric person who wants in this way to stretch his potentialities to the limit and take pleasure in them. This conflict is not a moral game for diversion. It is a state charged with special meaning. Let us consider Hamlet from the more recent world of the tragic. The Danish prince does not himself provoke the dreadful crisis that will prove fatal for him. It comes of its own accord and finds him unsuspecting at Wittenberg, as do his mother's sin and his father's sudden death and, later, the command from Hades. After this, the hero's drama follows the path by which he responds to his circumstances and struggles against his outer and inner shackles.

A struggle against shackles — let us note this. Though it is nothing new, it may light the way in our further search. But let us proceed to the two heroes of Sophocles we have chosen. Oedipus is one of the most brilliant examples, because while he himself sets the drama in motion with his strong will, at the same time he appears enmeshed in dreadful oracles from before, from the time he was in swaddling clothes. A superficial eye would consider Laius' son condemned to do what he does, suffer what he suffers. It has been said that *Oedipus Tyrannus* is the "tragedy of fate." A more careful and unprejudiced examination — we will see this in greater detail in the following chapter — convinces us that the play is not the illustration of an oracle. The god foretells, knows the future, does not condemn — here is hidden the first half of the play's secret. The other half we shall examine as our inquiry proceeds. But even the first half of the secret is enough to show us that the poet chose the hero's will for the lever of the action. Thus on the purely dramatic plane, that is, on the plane of action, the human plane, the initiative belongs entirely to Oedipus. It is he who conducts the interrogation and discovers and pays. An unique example of initiative.

The other example, also from Sophocles, is Oedipus' daughter, Antigone. If I choose Antigone and not Electra, the reason is, I think, very obvious: Electra, in spite of her indomitable will, is a sick soul. Passionate, humiliated, she pines away waiting for her brother who will compensate her for the loss of her father-protector and for her sacrificed life. There is none of this in Antigone. With unclouded mind Oedipus' daughter advances to the fulfillment of a duty which she believes to be sacred, and which is unselfish. This, her firm conviction, and her unbending ethos make her passion appear rather cold in comparison to Electra's. What Antigone gains in moral stature she loses in dramatic intensity; just as the fiery Electra risks on the plane of moral purity what she gains in wild beauty. The economy of the drama has its own logic: one cannot be both passionately enough involved *and* unblemished. Antigone is blameless enough to hold her will upright and naked, a flashing sword.

I come to Euripides' heroine, this outermost boundary of madness: Medea. A barbarian herself, she has passed through the filter of a Greek tragic poet in order to be dramatized. What gives us the impression here of the existence of a free will is the fact that Medea uses her intellect intensely. Her soul may be dark, but her mind functions very clearly, with such logical precision that it nearly scandalizes us. Medea ponders, converses, argues; she has apparently been schooled in the era of dialectics' intellectual climate, if not that of the sophists. In spite of her saying that "Passion is stronger than plans" (1079).

Moreover, her initiative is founded on another basis, a historical one: she is the pioneer who demands the rights of her sex. From the theatrical aspect her initiative is emphasized by the virtually soliloquous character of the play. Jason, Creon, Aegeus are shadows around her. The tragedy *Medea* is the character Medea.

What has this brief documentation yielded us? We are searching for the tragic; that is why we have focused on plays that project a strong personality at their center. Not plays with a collective hero, like *The Persians*, *The Suppliant Maidens*, *The Trojan Women*. The five heroes we have seen are different from each other in their characters and in the circumstances of their lives. Are they perhaps related in some way? Certainly; each has a strong will. Prometheus, who defied the authority of the highest of the gods, has it; Eteocles, who laid down his life to defend his fatherland although he knew he was marked by Fate, has it; Oedipus, who disregards whether he will pay for his inquisitive thirst for truth, has it; Antigone, who defies the political authority for the sake of a law in which she believes blindly, has it; Medea, who, in order to satisfy a corrosive passion, lacerates the deepest root of her sex, has it. All these strong wills come into conflict with an order of things that is actually stronger. All five pay dearly for adherence to their cause. Thus far, I would say these essential elements are known.

But when I delve into the specific circumstances of these tragic heroes, when I attempt to elevate myself above their confluent elements, I surmise that something else, something strange, touches me. These five human types, one might say, convey not merely the burden of their fate, the conflict with an opposing order of values, they also in some way provoke it. Not by their *hamartia*, as Aristotle wishes it. Not by some action or negligence of theirs. Not by an inflexibility inherent in them; but by something else, externally hard to discern, logically inexplicable, which appears to draw Heaven's wrath inexorably upon them. To draw the thunder. It is as if their stars, their idiosyncrasies, willed it so. They have been born tragic, *they are born for tragedy.*

It seems prosaic to assume that Prometheus is crushed because he contended with the Olympians, or Oedipus with the will of the god who had spoken through the oracles. Prometheus is crushed because he is Prometheus, Oedipus because he is Oedipus. This means that the formidable force leading them to catastrophe is intrinsic to their character. But for more recent instances of the tragic genre, we must turn to the fortuitous, the arbitrary and unintelligible, to find an answer. We say, as Bradley says about the Shakespearian heroes: What fate willed that Othello would have Iago for his ensign and Lear daughters like Goneril and Regan? Or — we may add to Bradley — Macbeth his wife? Conclusion: the tragic hero, as if all the rest were not enough, is also terribly unlucky.

If we continued like this, we would not ask, according to Bradley, why Juliet woke up a minute too late, but what fate willed Romeo to meet the daughter of the Capulets — because this is the critical incident, as we shall see later, not the feud between the Capulets and the Montagues. Was it necessary, more than anything else, for the paths of the two "star-crossed" children of Verona to converge? And is Romeo "unlucky"? On the contrary, allow me to consider him enviably lucky. When one has the awesome privilege of being born a tragic hero (of being born for tragedy) one's form is not completed, one's existence is not perfected, except with the aesthetic fulfillment that is one's catastrophe. Aesthetic and tragic, here, become one, just as climax and catastrophe become one. What would Romeo be without a Juliet? Hamlet without his family misfortune? Oedipus without the riddle of the Sphinx and hubris? Antigone without the unburied body of Polyneices? Prometheus without fire? Most simply, they would not exist. These beings are not actual persons, they have been born for *this*, and only this, purpose; otherwise, they are inconceivable. Not that without their trials the myth would not exist; the *source* of the myth would not exist. "Myth" here means the realization of the hero's form and destiny.

It seems, then, that an inexplicable economy is manifested before our eyes: some hidden order of things brings forth, one could say, the beings necessary to reveal it, and, again, *they are irresistibly drawn* toward it, they rush to meet their fate with a kind of unrestrained, intoxicating passion. The tragic hero has in his psychosynthesis something pioneering, an unconscious urge toward the climax that will be his dramatic culmination and at the same time his ruin. Like the noble horse that bites his bit to rush on, even toward the precipice, to fulfill his true nature in the vertigo, he finds his mission only in the utmost intensity, in an aesthetic category, if not an ontological one.

We often speak, with respect to tragic heroes, about a "love for the absolute" that possesses them, and we shelter under this heading passions like those of Prometheus or Faustus, Oedipus or Romeo, Medea or Macbeth. The term is not inept, but it is hardly applicable in all cases. What is the passion for the absolute in Medea or Macbeth? Jealousy and ambition? The identity with one single purpose? The deception — if we use Christian precepts — by

Satan? It is difficult — for the moment at least — to name the passion for the absolute, negative, soul-destroying tendencies. They do not especially convince us that they lie at the center of the picture. If Medea were merely the illustration of woman's jealousy in its utmost form, and Macbeth the representation of an ambition that, in the midst of disaster like the one that ensues, results in sheer vainglory, we would have psychological dramas, not tragedies. We have tragedies because, after a certain point, we realize that passion in these situations is the pretext for something much more profound, more enigmatic, to be suggested to us: a dangerous spirit — a force of unbridled Evil in the world — which is localized in beings susceptible to it and which has made them the vessels of its choice.

Thus the tragic hero appears imbued with a strange passion, an unconscious impulse that compels him to pursue his destination, his fulfillment, through catastrophe. This salient trait distinguishes him strikingly from other men, endows him with something particular, something that is inspiring and preordained. It does not matter whether this trait is related to distinctions of the social or intellectual type: royal crown, political power, noble birth, intellectual stature. All kings are not fit to be tragic heroes nor all conquerors or all men with an insatiable thirst for knowledge. A spirit of innate anxiety seems to imbue those born for tragedy, a hidden demon spurs them on, even when they at first appear calm before our eyes, like Lear or Othello. The crisis of the drama, when it breaks out, will suddenly unleash the agony, whereas a human being not born to be a tragic hero will compromise, will come to terms. If he finds himself in Oedipus' place he will act with slackness, or try to strangle the truth; in Antigone's, withdraw into seclusion lamenting Polyneices; in Juliet's, weep, then yield and marry Paris; in Hamlet's, commit suicide or become a misanthropic anchorite or instigate an uprising to topple Claudius and seize the throne. These are the actions of common men. But Prometheus lets himself be bound on the Caucasus and Othello does not forgive Desdemona but smothers her. Not that they have fallen into *hamartia* as Aristotle wants, but because they have been born solely and exclusively for this purpose: to give cosmological meaning to the cause they serve. Only thus do they "exist." The tragic spirit is relentless. Like the legendary bird, it becomes intoxicated in the storm.

This predisposition, this innate tendency toward ruin and suffering, which is not masochistic, this I call the tragic spirit. It is an ontological category. It contains a magnitude, regardless of whether it is moral or aesthetic: the moral, here, acquires an aesthetic value, and the aesthetic acquires moral authority. It is necessary to distinguish it from the external confluence of circumstances in social life that occasionally brings ordinary men to situations that are seemingly analogous to those of the tragic heroes. Every man who slays his wife is not an Othello, nor is every ideologue who loses the game and must pay the price a Brutus or a Prometheus. What, in everyday life, makes the usage of the terms "tragic" and "tragedy" inappropriate is precisely this ignorance of the hero's organic involvement in the crucial event. In life, we call tragic what crushes, we do not call tragic what does not exist without being destroyed; for the very simple reason that life's mission is blind preservation. And this shows us at once why only in the realm and the jurisdiction of the aesthetic can the tragic spirit be conceived.

"That which does not exist without being crushed."

Indeed, the concept of the tragic spirit leads us, if we delve deeply into it, beyond the narrow space of the theatrical. The tragic is not only a concept, it is also a life experience; it is an inextricable tangle of life experience and concept. The difficulty in pinpointing it is due to the fact that we have to deal with a purely existential concept, which only in a second phase finds a logical formulation. To answer why the tragic hero is so created as to attract the thunder is difficult and perhaps futile. Once more, with the tragic we touch a more remote realm that does not tolerate the intervention of typical logic. We speculate only that here a coincidence is expressed, or that the figure of the pre-ordained man is as we said above: something like a vessel of choice, but of unrelenting choice, with inhuman demands.

Thus we pass on to the other relationship that characterizes the tragic, the feeling of some fundamental antinomy: man proclaims man as the highest value, but the physical universe treats him with an indifference unbecoming the preeminence it appears to have granted him. It seems like contempt. When one transcends the level of common everyday submission, one arrives at insights that at first evoke bewilderment, then revolt, and finally doubt, resulting in catastrophe. It is as though two omnipotent wills came into collision — one eponymous, one anonymous; one concrete, one abstract, one obvious, one hidden. The inability to localize the enemy is not one of the least significant features of tragedy. It is equally vague in *Oedipus* or *Macbeth*, *Antigone* or *Othello*. Because the real enemy is impersonal; he is *hidden* behind the characters, whether good-intentioned or insidious: behind Creon as well as Iago. It is a will with an unverifiable, obscure identity.

A tall tale? Not at all. We live in a given universe, which has not revealed to us its raison d'être. We accept it exactly as given, and this is, essentially, the only thing we know about its truth and its meaning. When we compromise, we speak of materialism and realism; when astonished, we speak of spiritualism and idealism. To conform or disagree is all we are given. But the fact is not refuted that there is no ground for basic choice. Existence in this universe, and not in any other, has been imposed upon us in an irrefutable way. It is upon this compulsory service that the miracle relies. It concerns a dream which we cannot choose or control or be free to escape or know the meaning of. And even this: whether we believe in it or not, the terms do not change. It has enlisted us in its dance in absentia — a brief presence, right in the midst of our eternal absence.

But why the obligatory affinity of the tragic hero with the terms, the conditions of tragedy? Does such acceptance mean fatalism or naïve romanticism? In fact, the Romantic theater of the beginning of the nineteenth century had invented such a type of hero, the *maudit*, who seems to be nothing but a sentimental variation on the preordained man we are talking about. Schiller's youthful heroes, especially Don Carlos, and Victor Hugo's heroes — Hernani, Ruy Blas — project this model. They are an extension of the Byronic hero with a past already burdened (Manfred is the prototype) with the presentiment of a condemnation, with the keenest, most tormenting sensitivity. What is the relationship of this romantic type to the hero imbued with the tragic spirit? Could he be a simplification, a rationalized variation of the latter?

To some extent, yes; but only to the extent that justifies the appearances. Because the tragic spirit is different in substance from the romantic: it does not aim at pathos. The tragic spirit is harsh toward itself, ascetic, not narcissistic. In no instance does it give the impression that it is looking at itself from without, in order to adore the plastic stance it has assumed in life.

What explains its predisposition toward catastrophe? Some morbid inclination? Not at all! The inability perhaps to bear the revelation of a hidden and dreadful truth? Exactly the opposite! The tragic spirit tends irrevocably toward the ultimate confrontations because it is inflamed by what is marginal, unattainable, unbearable, ineffable, beyond the conventional standards of everyday life. On the plane of knowledge it gives us Prometheus, as later it will give us Marlowe's Faustus; on the plane of moral duty, Eteocles and Antigone; on the plane of truth, Oedipus. I regret I cannot add Medea to the list, but the moment has come to say this: Euripides is responsible for all the great concessions. Euripides introduced pathos into the theater, that is, the passion that takes pleasure in looking at itself. Since pathos was without precedent in a robust world, it induced Aristotle to characterize Euripides as the "most tragic of poets."

This epithet, instead of redeeming Euripides, does an injustice to Aristotle, at least insofar as tragedy is concerned. The condemnation of Euripides, however, lies in his division, a dismemberment between pathos and sophistic dialectics. The one results in the irony of the other, a fact the poet of the *Medea* seems not to have suspected, despite all his Athenian sharpness of mind.

The tragic spirit is intensely aware that a threat is incessantly suspended, like a sword, over man's life. Thus it is metaphysically conscious, but without being panic-ridden. It has the awareness that an abyss is yawning be-

neath our feet — as Pascal felt it. In the classical scale and
mode it is formulated — in numerous passages — by Aeschylus in *The Libation Bearers* in the voice of the Chorus:

> *No mortal shall pass his life to the end*
> *unscathed, without paying for it.*
>
> (1017–1018)

Sophocles defines it in *Oedipus Tyrannus*, in the famous
chorus passage:

> *Alas, generations of mortals,*
> *I count your life*
> *as equal to zero.*
>
> (1186–1188)

The realm of tragedy is the realm of the utterly dangerous, where pretexts, all the delusions of life, collapse. Who
has not noticed how Attic tragedy hastens to arrive at the
lamentation? It often appears to have been wrought exclusively and solely around a lamentation that lies at its
very center, if it is not its main theme. One explanation
may be historical: that tragedy began from the choral lamentation and later radiated into the dramatic genre. The
other explanation, however, is the aesthetic, which contains a metaphysical explanation: that tragedy means a
play which deals with an immediate, intuitive awareness
of ultimate threat, formulates it and records it.

The tragic spirit has on its lips the taste of the abyss.
Where the ordinary man is fooled with illusions and suc-
cumbs to the ephemeral aspects of life, the tragic hero has
been formed so as to incline toward what will make him

suddenly see beyond the illusionary, the consoling, and the necessary.

A strange strength characterizes him, even when at some point in his dramatic progress we see him temporarily bend. The tragic spirit is born for unrelenting vigilance. It knows, sees, perceives a dark presence at the crucial core of life. It lives through feeling what is incurably exposed. Philoctetes expresses this at a certain moment in his simple language, bare in its directness:

> ... you save me, you pity me, seeing
> how mortals are always dangerously exposed
> to both fortune and misfortune.
> Whoever is without afflictions should beware of danger
> and when he lives in happiness, should watch
> most closely, lest his life be ruined unawares.
>
> (501–506)

At this point another concept appears and burdens the awareness of the tragic: evil. It is as vague a term as it is terrifyingly concrete. Let us consider it in all its aspects, as both physical and moral evil, as metaphysical scandal even. It intensifies the incomprehensible as well as the abusive, which the ephemeral, that is, death, and the vanity of all things assume in our eyes. It is not accidental that the ancient tragic poets were born in a still-dawning era, that they were nearer to primitive fears. Aeschylus, and Sophocles, too, give us the impression at moments of communicating with the chaos which existed before the appearance of human life in the world, that chaos which, although it is exposed, is not necessarily abolished. It always looms, threatening, beyond the appeasing façade of things.

Let us not forget that the same observation — strange
as it seems — has been made about Shakespeare. The famous lines of Othello are often quoted:

> But I do love thee! And when I love thee not,
> Chaos is come again.
>
> (Othello, III, iii, 91–92)

Alas if we take these lines as a rhetorical figure or an
outburst of grandiloquence. This plain soldier knows
nothing about grandiloquence; his blood is behind every
word. In back of Othello's conviction looms the threat of
chaos, and the only raft the tragic spirit has at its disposal
for remaining afloat is its confidence in moral purity.
When this sensitive instrument collapses, the hero sinks
to the depths. The play is an experiment showing that
the only thing worthwhile in this world of destructive con-
tradictions is man's grandeur, the inner grandeur deso-
lately symbolized in the greatness of the hero.

Thus we pass on, inevitably, to the plane of aesthetics.
We said above that a Prometheus would be inconceivable
without fire, an Antigone without disobedience to the law
of the state, an Oedipus without errors and hubris. What
does this mean? That these persons, more than characters,
are actions. Indeed, each one of them is one main, central
action. They exist in relation to this action; they exist for
it. They have been born solely and exclusively for the
dimensions of the drama, the stage space. The tragic hero
is understood only in the categories of the aesthetic. This
simple observation brings us to other questions.

The tragic spirit is a concept beyond the reality of practical life, intelligible only as a poetic notion. Does it perhaps contain a value to counterbalance what is lacking in

our life? But then where does its authority lie? In the effort perhaps to beautify an organic weakness of ours? Do we perhaps conceive of the tragic as thought and as category because we are unable to experience it?

The question — let us say so at once — poses a pseudoproblem. We raise it here only out of methodological expediency. On the aesthetic plane we project the deeper purified tendencies of our practical life. If the tragic spirit completes itself poetically only on the aesthetic plane, this does not mean that it comes into antithesis with our experience, that it constitutes a falsehood, however devout. We would not recognize something alien to our inner experience as our own, no matter how it flattered us. We recognize it — not even with our minds, but with our guts — because it projects something idealized which is, therefore, our *real* longing, something we nourish with our heart's blood. What is this thing? That will be our last question.

But first let us gather together the characteristics of the tragic spirit we have been able to clarify. It is, we have said, a struggle against shackles, against the feeling of an impasse. Then it is the pioneering, the innate inclination toward the painful spasm leading to a dreadful revelation. It is, finally, a state of fundamental antinomy: man, the highest value in his own eyes, vs. the order of the world which ignores him or plots against him, and in any case crushes him. Do these three components possibly create a synthesis that makes them communicate with each other? I think so: the will to bring about a reconnoitering confrontation between man and the world. A confrontation whose purpose is not to increase or promote our knowledge, but to illustrate some other territory within us, a dark zone.

The tragic feeling and revelation does not inform us: it provides us with a profound experience. What is elevated within us is not our reasoning; it is the existential ethos. I call it this to distinguish it from the social ethos, which is conventional. Tragedy does not inspire self-confidence, although a peculiar euphoria inundates the soul. It brings before our eyes certain prototypes, personages born to approach the outermost realm of the tolerable, to live dreadful experience. These personages, idealized by the aesthetic process, become worthy of evoking wonder in us and even something like a strange, fleeting envy: If only we resembled them . . . This thought leaves us breathless, for it is frightening to resemble a hero of tragedy. The tragic emotions of pity and fear — attention here! — should not be considered separately, but as something composite. They are not two, but one. To the tragic hero, because of what he proves himself capable of experiencing, we accord the right to represent us, the privilege of expressing us. He is the bearer of our silent command.

Of all things what do we mòst envy in him? His grandeur and beauty. An invisible beauty, which is not only the transubstantiation of his moral stance into a plastic one, for sometimes it may resemble the opposite of moral beauty, as in the case of a great sinner: a Medea, a Macbeth or a Richard. This beauty consists of an exultation in the life force, a passionate intensity which is consumed by its own flame. It elevates the tragic hero to a strange human prototype, it opens for him potentialities beyond the ordinary, which terrify us. But is it not in precisely this awesomeness, this feeling that we are approaching a realm bordering on the abyss, that we have witnessed the overwhelming vertigo of tragedy? On the contrary: a realm where everything would be subject to restoration, if only human law functioned differently, if institutions were consequential, would constitute — and does constitute — a realm of the dramatic, not of the tragic. The tragic begins at the border beyond which nothing can be remedied; it is the realm where, behind institutions, uninstituted laws rise. It is *necessary* for Creon's law to govern the cities, the organized human societies, and it is *necessary* for Antigone to come into conflict with this law. Tragedy means an ontological antinomy.

That is why it does not lead to solution, but to catastrophe. The tragic hero rises to his climactic point one second before he falls forever. Within us, then, something profound is stirred, intoxicated, and this rapture is not solely moral or aesthetic. It is something composite that fills us with exultation and euphoria. We do not ask of the tragic hero that he be faultless; we ask of him the greatness that will evoke and sustain our admiration. In his deception, his defeat, his suffering, what we are asking from him is dignity. The tragic dignity becomes the foundation for the aura of grandeur.

"Let what will burst forth," cries Oedipus before he is destroyed. "I yearn to know my birth, however humble it may be" (1076–1077).

And Macbeth:

> I 'gin to be aweary of the sun,
> And wish the estate o' the world were now undone.
> Ring the alarum bell! Blow, wind! come, wrack!
> At least we'll die with harness on our back.
>
> (V, v, 49–52)

Courage here seems to counterbalance the hero's errors. The aesthetic compensates for the moral. We have only to think that if Macbeth had died a coward, we would hiss him in the theater — he would not be a hero worthy of tragedy, even if he had suffered all that he suffered.

If I wanted now to conclude with an epitome of what we have enumerated, if I were to attempt to name the elements that characterize the tragic spirit, I would suggest the predisposition of the tragic hero and the affirmed antithesis of man with the world order. I should perhaps speak of the *moral* order of the world, but I do not like to discuss unverifiable matters. His predisposition causes the tragic hero to advance, in some way or with some pretext, toward the realm of the utterly dangerous. The antithesis affirms that the outcome of his adversity will certainly be harsh. Even in tragedies with seemingly happy endings, the antithesis is not invalidated. It is always a deus ex machina who brings about a reconciliation, a dictated compromise, who finds a certain modus vivendi that ensures the coexistence from this point on. Such is the case in Aeschylus' *The Libation Bearers*, of *Iphigenia in Tauris*, and of *Medea*.

If this did not happen, if in the end there dawned a glimpse of hope that everything had been founded upon a misconception, if the hero had been allowed, even at the last moment, to hope, then the spectacle of the crucial conflict would be only a deception, something like a plot of the gods aimed at the beguilement of man. The meaning would no longer be located in this world. It would be in the "other world," where we would know truth reigns.

But the world of tragedy affirms that it is the only world with authority, and that is why the loss of this world is irreparable, and the lament for it inconsolable. The world of tragedy is the Greek world. In contrast with the Christian world, which promises redemption and eternity, the tragic world does not offer these possibilities, nor the consoling flight to the world beyond, nor any escape from reality. In the tragic world the hero has only one potentiality: to fulfill himself through his own danger, to drain the glass of his destiny to the very dregs. To become engulfed by his own flame.

What justification can there be in this? The answer is given us, through the isolation of the tragic hero, in the concept which has now emerged: dignity, in its special, tragic meaning. In creating a personal value of a third degree, humane, beyond the aesthetic and beyond the moral. Ephemeral like man. A value fulfilling itself through its destruction.

The tragic spirit, in this sense, is what places dignity higher than hope.

II

Savior Delian Paean!

. . . he kept on searching for his identity.
— Plutarch, *Moralia*

IT IS NOW NECESSARY to enter the very realm of tragedy. For it is there that the tragic spirit is realized. Tragedy is *the action*, in the fundamental sense, just as the Gospel pronounces "in the beginning was the Word" and Goethe's Faust, a man fragmented internally, the child of the Enlightenment, wonders whether "in the beginning was the deed."

To penetrate into the tragic play it would be preferable not to begin with theoretical generalities but to attempt a more immediate and warmer contact with the body of tragedy; even then we must choose from the multitude of types available in the ancient drama. Preferably, we need a play which is a kind of epitome of the tragic in its purest form. An epitome not so much as a summation of virtues but as a condensation of characteristics with specific meaning. We need a play combining the dramatic qualities of the tragic along with its pure intellectual substance.

I shall avoid tragedies forming parts of a trilogy, because their testimony, for that very reason, often becomes misleading. The balance of values in them is interwoven with the general design in the economy of the whole. From Sophocles, who wrote single, not "complicated," tragedies, I think no one will be surprised if I choose *Oedipus Tyrannus.*

As a rule, *Oedipus Tyrannus* is chosen because it is the prototype of dramaturgy. But our viewpoint here is different. Without overlooking the structural perfection of the play, I mean without avoiding its brilliance whenever it is helpful, we shall begin with the thought that what distinguishes *Oedipus Tyrannus* is its hidden nature. *Oedipus Tyrannus* consists of testimonies which, although not absent from other tragic plays of the ancient theater, in no other play converge so focused, so well balanced, and at the same time so enigmatic. This last point intensifies the intellectual charm and authenticity of the tragedy of Laius' son.

There is a mystery in *Oedipus Tyrannus*, but not the one apparent at first glance. What is apparent — the enigma of the *miasma* (pollution), the question of fate, the three oracles, the incest, the parricide, the preordination — does not express the meaning. But how then shall we approach the play? Should our viewpoint be that of our era and of its criteria? Or should we make an effort to establish a closer contact with the very ancient substratum contemporaneous with the poet, if not antecedent to him? To detach ourselves from our world is not easy, we know that; and again, it is hard to diagnose, and harder even to experience, what Sophocles believed, knew, and felt. Yet to ignore this aspect would be three times worse. The problem thus formulated provides us with nothing new, becomes more difficult here because we aim at the heart of the tragic and not at interpretation, morphological or philological, of this or that dramatic work.

In such instances one should exhaust all the means at one's disposal. It is the only thing one can do. Provided these means are not conventional. We need to sharpen our sensibility, evoke our intuition — that slandered, shriveled concept — and at the same time remain ruthlessly alert. Finally, the mind should be as well informed as possible. With this we have more or less announced the determining presuppositions of our course. We now have to muster the courage not to retreat.

Whoever encounters *Oedipus Tyrannus* for the first time wonders what Sophocles wanted to say in this play. *Electra* or *Antigone* does not compel us to think in these terms. Their myths, as developed and illuminated by the action, appear self-sustaining: Electra lives with the dream of revenging her unjustly slain father, and she finally succeeds; Antigone defends with her life a principle she believes is higher than the expediency of political power. The outcome in these cases is the matching counterbalance of the demand. But why does Oedipus suffer all the dreadful things he suffers although consciously he has done no wrong? On the contrary, has he not done whatever he could not to sin? There is something of a scandal here.

Starting with this question, one risks propounding another interpretation of the play amid the great number that have been put forth. What will rescue us here, I hope, is the difference of aim. We do not attempt to solve the riddle of Oedipus; we only want to search for the elements of the tragic at its authentic source. This means that we shall stop whenever we feel we have reached that seething raw substance. However, if some interpretive elements spring forth occasionally we shall not ignore them.

The first of Oedipus' characteristics that catches the eye immediately is the very special nature of his case. It is hard to dramatize a person who has killed his father and married his mother. It is difficult not because he is defiled, as Aristotle would say, judging outside the play's framework, but because at its starting point it formulates an exception that touches upon the boundaries of the improbable. However, without viewing verisimilitude as a statistical measurement, we need to distill from the characteristic elements of a myth some more or less typical human traits; only then is our participation evoked. Electra's revenging passion and her wounded feeling of justice, or Antigone's ideological irreconcilability, express familiar human feelings. Personally, Oedipus does not even appear governed by feelings, at least not until he is brought to his knees. He seems governed by an external, arbitrary, annihilating fate. That is why his tragedy is called a "tragedy of Fate." *Oedipus Tyrannus*, according to the established notion, is the tragedy of fate par excellence. Even more than the story of Orestes.

There is only one way to dramatize such a myth: his exploration must have revealed a hidden meaning to the poet. Will this meaning be man's destructive dependence on the inexplicable or arbitrary will of the gods? Will it be something different, more personal and enigmatic? No matter what, the eccentric character of the myth is dispelled only when the meaning it discloses presents an extreme case, which because of its hyperbole symbolizes something below the surface, the triviality, the commonplace of life. Then the pattern of events is surpassed, the improbable becomes a sort of revealing sign of a further truth. The mythological becomes humanized, or rather, the human is elevated to a mythic dimension — and, through this, to a metaphysical dimension as well.

That Sophocles is a poet determined by a religious disposition we know well from his entire oeuvre, or from the small but representative part of it which is extant and bears witness to his unrecorded life as well. The germane point about the religiousness of the ancient poets is that it did not serve a theologically formulated doctrine. This is of paramount importance, and we should keep it in mind. Not only is the ancient poet's consciousness left free to move amid the world of symbols which, without exception, embody — for him, as for any genuinely religious spirit — all the phenomena of this world; not only is he unbound by any codex of rules and forms; on the contrary, he believes that his objective is to provide an explanation for the inexplicable. This is a responsible explanation, because it is personal, not dictated, but affirmed by the import of the life of the man who has signed it. In this sense the ancient poet is a "hierophant," as many like to call him. He has nothing in common with certain latter-day examples, people who claim the charisma of the Illuminati to set themselves apart from the uncouth masses.

Is it too daring perhaps to believe that in the case of Oedipus Sophocles studied the myth in depth in order to construct his play? To believe the opposite would be an impertinence: to suppose the only problem that occupied the poet was the skillful handing of his material. That is why the excellent structure of *Oedipus* should not obscure its inner meaning. The structure of *Oedipus* springs forth organically from the meaning of the play. It is this which makes its structure so solid and definitive.

What is its dynamic form, Bergson might have asked. The search for an unknown being. In the first phase, a man strives to discover an unknown culprit. In the second phase, the one who conducts the interrogation realizes that the person wanted is he himself. The first and definitive theme we have in *Oedipus Tyrannus* is the persistent quest for identity.

At no instant should we forget this result of the play, which is so obvious anyway. The daring of the poet relies on the invisible but also inevitable transportation of the target. The defendant and the prosecutor are the same person. This reversal could be either a plot device or a revealing sign. The one excludes the other; that is why it is almost always forgotten that the latter determines the former. If the opposite had happened, *Oedipus Tyrannus* would be a drama of suspense.

But the play's religious tone, viewed through the emotional experience of our world, through our categories, is likely to mislead us again. For us a play of religious inspiration, when it is not an unraveling of an exemplary myth or an outburst of mysticism, is an allegory with didactic overtones. Calderón — the typical example of a religious dramaturge of the Christian world — shows this eloquently. The Morality plays of the medieval theater, revived with only less naïveté now in the contemporary theater, make clear what we mean. In *Oedipus Tyrannus* neither alternative exists. That is why I dread the characterization "a play of religious inspiration," although I am unable to avoid it.

We must be very careful, for it is not at all accidental that a most powerful human figure is found at the center of the picture Sophocles has composed. An allegorical play almost never has anything similar to show. Kafka's heroes are abstractions comparable to allegorical figures;

they are not specific human beings. They look like scuba suits which, because anyone can wear them, thus assume the generality hidden in their design. But Oedipus, before revealing himself to be anything else, constitutes a person with definite — in fact terrifyingly, inescapably definite — identity. As has been correctly observed, his character is one of the most complex and fully developed in ancient tragedy.

For such a character to be conceived, something different from moral or analytical thinking is required. A powerful vibration is needed at the beginning. Everything in the complete play reveals that at a certain moment the poet seized the character of his hero from within the depths of the prerational, and brought it out into the light. I do not maintain that this happened by chance. On the contrary, I believe that such emergence occurs only after a headlong submergence; Sophocles has passionately studied the case of Laius' son, examined it painstakingly, and searched to find what might be hiding in this enigma of a marked life: where it diverges from the fate of other men, where it converges, and why. Is the adversity that gives it meaning independent of character, of the given personality? Does it come from the outside? Is it something that could happen to anyone? Or does there perhaps exist a dark, inexplicable correlation here between fate and personality? And, to recall the ideas of the first chapter, is an Oedipus born perhaps to attract the thunder upon himself, or does it appear so to us, a posteriori, because it happened so? And when we speak of *Ananke* (Necessity) do we thus mean the typical outcome of the action? Or do we mean a consequence of the challenge that a particular human existence, merely and simply because it exists, unconsciously directs to the Unknown? But then, is not an inexplicable preordination already projected here?

The man who lived such a life was prominent indeed! The myth itself indicates this. Behind the enigma of the Sphinx with its childlike mythical impression lies hidden another enigma, and the former is but the symbolic formulation of the latter. Is it the enigma of life? The enigma of the world? The enigma of the Unknown? The enigma of the enigma? They all fit here. One thing is important: that this enigma is death-bringing. Either you give the right answer or you are destroyed. If you solve it, you become a king. But even if you become a king, again, you are not saved: one day you will pay even more dearly than if you had not solved it.

The myth has depth, dimensions, like those in Genesis. Is it an archetypal myth perhaps, a remnant of immemorial, collective wisdom? In any case, it is not merely a fairy tale, not a one-dimensional and pleasant narrative. Nor must we search and decipher myth through methodical analysis. On the contrary, one can imbue it with whatever meaning one wishes, provided it is not arbitrary. It ensues from the reservoir of existential anguish; such myths are like equations: they give the formula, not the conclusions.

Oedipus the solver of the Sphinx's enigma was already a prominent figure, even without his encumbered heredity. Anyway, the preordination here, the initial oracle to Laius, does nothing more than foretell the bare outlines of the child to come. The monsters and signs, the future parricide and incest, are tangible images announcing a monstrous birth. In order to solve the riddle of the Sphinx, the riddle of the riddle that man is, one must be born a violator of the natural law, an upsetter of the unsuspecting balance, an apostate. To maintain peace in society, it is better that such children be sent to be devoured by the wild beasts of Cithaeron. But again, their own monstrous fate protects them. It does not release them from its claws before it says what it has to say.

Within the framework of the ancient religious soul, such a myth is religious, because it contains the elements par excellence of the religious: the incomprehensible and the awesome. It is, furthermore, religious because it allows freedom of choice. It depends on you to give it voice, to dare its decipherment. The religious firmament for the ancient conscience is an unfathomable realm, a domain that rouses; it is not a restrictive codex. Hence the awe — a typical reaction of the ancient religious soul — in contrast to the latter-day appeasing piety. Despite its anthropomorphic expression, ancient pantheism contains something restless; it is not tamed as is humanized Christian theism.

Oedipus in the first given of the myth is already an exceptional figure, by his position. For him to become exceptional also by nature, the intuition of a poet is needed. Sophocles will bring this about; he will bestow the chrism. The play, from this point on, instead of becoming an attempt to decipher a myth, becomes the decipherment of a human life. The difference is significant, because from the abstract we have now crossed over to the plane of the concrete; from the figural to the plastic. From a fleshless idea to warm blood. Sophocles bending down to explore, to confess the fate of a man of both intellectual and tragic stature, is a theme by its nature full of empathy: man looks within man, reaches out to penetrate the barrier of the unknown, to see behind the silent façade even if he is bound to draw the veil of Maya. If behind the veil looms the glance of the Medusa, Oedipus is not the only one to see it; Sophocles will see it too. From here on, the hero and the poet share the same fate. Tragedy becomes the supreme human experience, a first skirmish at the border of Hades. The Sphinx that killed herself did not withdraw: she has left her glance transfixed, suspended before the star-studded firmament.

Here, in order to come down directly to the reality of the theater, which in no way should ever escape us, we must bear in mind something that our contemporaries inevitably forget, both in the theater and in reading the play. Today we see the ancient plays performed with the faces of the actors unmasked. But even when the staging makes an effort to refer to the sources of the theater and uses masks again, the impression of today's spectator bears no relation to that of the spectator in the ancient theater. The mask for us, especially with the dimensions and expressions of classical times, appears somewhat odd. For the ancient spectator the oddity would be an actor's bare face. Today a mask impresses at first and is quickly forgotten. It becomes a prop. Its psychological mechanism in the fifth century B.C. must have been quite different. Its first manifestation was the transference of the spectator to a plane other than that of an ordinary experience. This inner domain is nonexistent today; the transference therefore takes place in a vacuum.

Without intending to elaborate upon this point, which appears somewhat superfluous to our main topic, and without insisting by these few remarks that we should use or not use masks in contemporary interpretation, I shall limit myself to stressing not the difference between two interpretations, but between the two worlds. The ancient tragic hero who came into existence in the theater attained something indefinably mystical and grotesque. In form he may not have been remote from the human race, but he was remote from everyday man, from the ideal of our world. The tragic figure suspended between the divine and the human, between the theologeion and the orchestra, summarized, and in summarizing, revealed. Today to be able to approach Oedipus, Electra, or Antigone, we are compelled to expand the human. The ancient spectator, on the other hand, had to moderate the heroic in order to meet with the human.

The importance of this difference is that in ancient times half the distance had already been covered from the start. We dismount more easily from the cothurni than we mount them; we eradicate more easily than we elevate, and even more easily when the passions that begin unfolding before us reveal familiar weaknesses and therefore become more human. But a mask-bearing face has generality; it is a symbol, not an individual with a social identity. The accentuation of appearance to the point of grotesqueness reveals moods and tendencies of our inner world, exaggerated through the intensity that myth and passion provide. I see man through a magnifying glass, and this makes him grow like a giant, it shows him as terrifying, dangerous. Not that he was not so before; but I did not know it. A fly in a magnifying glass becomes a dreadful monster.

In the eyes of the public viewing ancient theater, Oedipus, even apart from his exceptional fate, was not a common man. In his person, as in Electra's, Antigone's, or Philoctetes', survived, though unconsciously, something of the sacred monster, the primitive totem that gathered the chiefs of the race together. From this point on, it is one step before we cross over into the realm of the holy.

The tragic hero, the tragic figure, has a secret and primitive holiness, although he treads on the human level. He is the bearer of a secret world of the depths, of powers, of demons, of metaphysical monsters.

For our world, which since the Renaissance has been scourged by realism, such a concept of the tragic hero is per se incomprehensible. Neither the poet nor the spectator can conceive of it. Unwittingly today we subtract a great deal from Oedipus, even as readers of the text. This not only distorts the hero, but also strips from the completeness of the play one of its essential dimensions. Probably the only thing accessible to us today is what resembles us, that is, what reminds us of each other. For us, something both probable and improbable, nearby and distant, something that conveys its own standards, would be incomprehensible.

It will be answered perhaps that the avant-garde theater succeeded in imposing on the public consciousness some grimacing, dehumanized beings. These beings, however, belong to a totally different order of values. They remove us even farther from the world of the ancient tragic characters. In today's theatrical characters exist the preconceived, the abstraction spurned by mockery, the aggressively impersonal, hence a disposition for criticism; whereas the ancient characters were endowed with exaltation of the personal and an admiring attitude toward it. Tragicomedy is not a variant of tragedy; it is its mockery. There is no similarity — although my good and otherwise marvelous friend Jan Kott wishes it so — between Beckett's Vladimir and Estragon and Shakespeare's King Lear, Fool, and Edgar. Tragicomedy can be, from one point of view, a new concept of the tragic; but it is not a new aspect of tragedy.

The fate and the predicament of a prominent man who

has come to life marked — these we see for the moment as the possible starting points of the poet. It seems that in these Sophocles searched to find a meaning. The meaning of the fate of one man and, through this, of Man. But when we say "fate" here, we do not mean Fate. The facile alibi of an intellectual complacency that surmises it has found the meaning and the law of tragedy in consigning them to an empty word is unacceptable. When we say "fate" we mean the riddle of a life. From this point to the riddle of Life the distance is but one step.

But let us examine the climate in which the play begins, its tonic, as they would say in music. I insist on this, because more or less all analyses, on the contrary, delve into the elements of the myth and the action.

The propylaea of a palace, an open space in front of it, the altar — a permanent symbol of worship — where still rises and unravels the last thread of smoke from the sacrifice that has taken place earlier. Two or three altars in front of the palace. And suddenly a din from the side, a swarm of people of every age rushes into the orchestra, falling on their knees before the altars, embracing them, huddling on the ground. They carry supplication branches, with bits of wool coiled around them. Backstage, far off, in the unseen city which has suddenly emerged in our imagination with the entrance of the crowd, the lamentations spread, multiply. A people beating their breasts.

From the first words of the figure — a troubled leader — who appears as the palace gate opens we learn many things. But first the atmosphere of the moment will be clarified.

I will not dwell on the external dramatic intensity of this opening scene. I will call attention to the inner "aroma" of the moment as it develops with the supplication of the priest who starts speaking. All ages are present,

from the "newly born bird" to those who stoop beneath
their years. But there are others, too, who enlarge the
picture: those who, as we hear, wander wreathed in mourning, at the marketplace, the temples, and the oracular altar
of Ismenus piled high with the ashes of victims. The
whole city "stirs," rocks like a ship in a destructive storm.
Evil omens: seeds wither in the earth, flocks of sheep die,
women bring to the light dead children. The "flame-
bearing god" has fallen upon the country and lays it waste,
feeding dark Hades with groans and lamentations. It is as
if the lamentations of the city mingling with the smell of
incense were sinking deep into the earth and shaking its
bowels.

At this point there is a choral ode. The scene in action
presented so far has, on the first level, a dramatic vividness which could be theatrically sufficient. On a second
level, however, the scene attains a further dimension:
what scourges the country is divine wrath. Three elements are gathered in a sheaf within the very first min-
utes of the hour: a king who — in that age — is also a
religious leader, a priest, a plague with the signs of divine
wrath.

This atmosphere, which provides the opening testimony, will dominate the play. It will not fade from our
senses until it is absorbed by its main fruit: the revealing
reversal of fortune of the crowned hero. This utterance
will be taken up shortly to be developed on another plane,
in another musical scale, by the Chorus. Whoever attempts
to descend to the root of tragedy in order to immerse himself in its deeper substance finds it hard to overlook the
domain of the religious. The religious in the special meaning it had for the ancient world.

*

For us today, religion is a system of formidably organized beliefs and forms of worship; the religious is a disposition to respond to this system. One could find something similar — from one point of view — in the ancient world, too, with the difference that one should not try to conceive through it the inner vibration, the peculiar mysticism rooted at the heart of the ancient religious sentiment. The unfortunate thing is that if there is evidence for the former, ancient religion, for the latter, its actual content, none exists. For philosophers and students of religion studying these phenomena, it is natural to arrive at conclusions from concrete evidence: written texts, inscriptions, certain myths, which they analyze into their composite elements and similarities in order thereby to read their symbolic language. It is clear, however, that none of this, no concrete evidence, has preserved the nascent emotion of the ancient mystical fervor. In this, as in all other very personal matters, the ancients have remained very secretive. And even when mainly through the language of their poets they allow something to be perceived, the transference into speech, the subjugation to the tyranny of writing, has created a new barrier, translucent as well as impenetrable. We do not have the necessary receptivity to listen to the whispering sounds of the ancient inner voice. Its wavelength is not ours.

In the Prologue to this book, I asked permission to be subjective. I wanted to avoid the restrictions and fetters of a scholarly method. The grace of that method lies in the fact that what it proposes each time is verified. My lack of grace is to seek refuge occasionally in what is personal and unverified. I do not propose this as a "solution from despair." I simply do not object to it. It is anyone's prerogative to accept it or not.

One day, as I was walking in the countryside, I suddenly found myself in front of something resembling a fresh green thicket. It was formed by dense bushes all around and an aged plane tree, with its branches bending over a small spring gushing quietly at its roots, babbling. The limpid water spread into a pool, then flowed away, a tiny brook. It was one of those spots that seemed to have been forgotten by men and living a life of its own, very ancient, secret, and serene.

I stood enchanted at the winding bank, as if before a miracle. A blessed calm was distilled within me. I stood there oblivious of myself for a short while, contemplating without thinking, gazing at the water, when something strange startled me. I looked around amazed. I suddenly had the impression that something was vibrating in the air, invisible yet very palpable; something glittering in the grass, in the water, everywhere; an impersonal presence.

And then I understood. For a few moments, with my mind fortunately numbed, I believed that a multitude of tiny spirits, cheerful demons fluttering in the air, in the green reflection, had animated the landscape, spurring everything to exist, to sing with closed mouths.

These spirits were not coming from the world after man's Fall, the one that knows Good and Evil. As I sensed them existing around me, they did not have a moral hypostasis; their essence — if I can express it thus — was the throbbing life, the playfulness, something beyond the natural, the useful, or the harmful, beyond our own expediency. They did not deny the Good because they did not know it. Their carefree existence was not a negation, it was an affirmation: something *this side* of the border, antecedent to knowledge. A world which had not been instructed in sin.

Naturally, all this began clearing in my mind when the mechanism of thought was set in motion again — too soon, alas! When the mind began recording, analyzing the sensation which had not yet faded. When the magic was dispelled, when I got away from the tiny spring, I was again an important person of the twentieth century. I was carrying within me thousands of tiny dead bodies, and the lancet of pure reason had started dissecting them with scholastic conscientiousness.

I can now sum up the conclusions of my inquiry, but I can no longer resurrect its phantasmagoria. Nor if I went back to the little spring could I find it again. It was revealed to me then because I was unsuspecting. I took it by surprise and it took me by surprise. If I went back, I would be carrying in me the categories of my world, its wisdom smelling of ashes, its irony which is deprivation, its arrogance. One day I will leave this world wiser but without having understood anything, neither how I lived nor why I lived. All that progress promised me it has taken back.

Let's start then, since we cannot do otherwise, to record whatever pure reason can perceive and express: The direct communication with the universe, which is the deep voice of the prehistoric soul, involves the genesis of what we conventionally call the pantheistic spirit. The divine appears profusely, and imbues the natural world; it is neither identified with it (idolatry), nor separate from it (theism). In its every morsel the natural world is, for the pantheistic spirit, the bearer of a god, a vessel of secret choice, a means for the manifestation of the divine.

Starting out from this point, we may hope that we will open some back door to reach our goal: an approach to the tragic. In the beginning was the divine, the feeling of its presence. Its relation to the human, to our categories and anxieties, was not classified then; it was always left open to discovery. Nothing was given by apocalypse. God and moral law, god and justice, god and man's fate, all were an unknown X. The constantly sought for. The poet, the philosopher, the thinker were the vanguard within Time; their task was to search for these relations.

The ancient dramatic poet is religious in this sense. He advances into the utmost territory and searches for the meaning of the beings behind the myths. It is not in a concrete language, in palpable, completed concepts that he searches. He proposes possibilities, instances, and implores the divine to manifest itself. The divine will reveal its presence at the opportune time, indirectly, with the light it will shed upon events, with the secret source of light, which will also determine the direction of the shadow. Every tragedy is also an "epiphany": a symbolic revelation of the divine.

And thus the questions posed are sometimes ethical, sometimes ontological. In exploring the myth, the poet explores the will of the divine. Through his personal responsibility he tries to find answers. Just as the oracular response is the answer of an oracle, so tragedy, in a rough form, is the answer of the divine. Equally as symbolic as the oracular response. The poet, "second to truth," but a truth more profound than the Platonic saying has suggested, utters an oracular response which, in its turn, calls for interpretation.

Two elements converge in tragedy: the archetype of the myth, which is its subject matter each time, and the prehistory of the typology latent at the root of its structure, the ritualistic element. For the ancient religious conscience, the metaphysical means the hidden soul of the physical.

When the ancient man said, "Olympus," or "Apollo," he meant the mountain or the person, and also the symbol. The two were inseparable in his perception. We mean either the one or the other, now the one, and now the other. For us this meaning has been irrevocably severed from the myth; the former has become matter, the latter convention. Thus we miss the third, the spiritual element, which remained alive thanks to the union of the other two.

Throughout the play *Oedipus Tyrannus*, we see Apollo as the overseer. We see this notion culminating at the end, like a musical theme bursting forth into a crescendo. For the moment, we find ourselves at the parodos: "Savior Delian Paean!" (154). This is one of the most profound, truly immemorial utterances of tragedy. It cannot be translated into contemporary language. I daresay it contains the quintessence of the tragic. What else is left to us except to close our eyes, sink deeply into our inner selves, and let this cry resound within us, that it may awake some shadows?

> *Fear darkens my mind*
> *   and I tremble all over with fright,*
> *Savior Delian Paean,*
> *I fear what debt you will demand*
> *again today or in future years.*
> *Tell me, O child of Golden Hope,*
> *   immortal Voice.*
>
> (153–157)

Let us hear it within us, both as a prayer and a supplication uttered at a moment of great calamity, when one feels that the very foundations of the world are shaking. Tragedy often compels us to seek refuge, no matter how obscure the way is, in the expectation of an ancestral echo.

III

The Impure Root and
the Perfectly Pure Light–I

THE ATMOSPHERE of the play's opening is, therefore, ritualistic: fumes of incense, priests, suppliants, a king cum religious leader, a god-sent plague, a crowd of people in despair embracing the altars, their heads wreathed, hurrying to fall on their knees before the sanctuaries of the city. On the second level, which with the voice of memory underscores the first level, there is a monster that, although defeated, may also have left its threat suspended like a curse. There is a solver of death-bringing riddles, and a formidable, immutable prophecy, hallowed by myth although not as yet mentioned. All in all, there is a sense of cosmological devastation behind the divine atmosphere.

At this point, we should recall analogous crises in plays of a later period: *Macbeth*, for example, or *Hamlet*. Both are authentic expressions of the tragic. In *Macbeth*, we suddenly open our eyes in the midst of a hellish disturbance of the natural balance in which everything, all the fundamental principles, have been overturned; the ugly has become beautiful, and the beautiful ugly. In *Hamlet* the night is contaminated; chilling gusts from the graves circulate in the air; something is about to be disclosed, some unholy act. On the bastions, the hearts of the guards are fear-stricken.

Is this accidental? Mere coincidence between the ancient play and the more recent ones? If we look more carefully, we will see this is not so. This disturbance of the foundations of the world is not an impressionistic element, a "theatrical device." It is a discernment and a secret pronouncement. The tragic does not appear as an isolated, private case, a crisis whose significance is demonstrated only on the social, ethical, or psychological plane. It is the indication of a deeper, terrifying disturbance, an antinomy that shakes the bowels of an indeterminable order of things. Yet, to our eyes, still tragedy appears essential to the world; to the world as an inseparable, natural, and ethical principle. In this deep stratum, morality, the natural, and the ethical are intermingled. We are not on the plane of codified morality, with its practical sanction. We are on the plane where conscience is recognized as an organic effluence and gradation of being, not as its logical contradiction.

If we delve now into the qualitative fiber of other tragic plays that bear the seal of the authentic, we will see that the same is true, although it is not always explicitly stated, as in *Oedipus*, *Hamlet*, or *Macbeth*. In the *Oresteia*, for instance, with the supernatural powers so immediately engaged in human affairs; where the blood shed within the palace of the Atreids, and steaming before it is smelled by Cassandra. In *Prometheus Bound*, with the clash of Titans and gods. In all Aeschylus' plays without exception. In Sophocles, whom we can now examine with a different, keener eye, an eye that can see beyond the narrow family circle. Dauntless Electra guards the shadow of a dead man, demanding blood. Antigone longs to restore a holy act that had been shaken and defiled. Philoctetes is both victim and exponent of an incurable sacred wound. Thus we see that the ancestral sin, the old debt, predestination, renowned "Fate" are not the devices of myths or of primitive superstitions. They are necessary, revealing indications of an antinomy that is intrinsic to the essence of being, that is pervasive, although it is veiled from common view by the harmony of the universe. Using this as criterion, we reflect now upon the authenticity of the tragic in another play, one of the more recent and loftier: *King Lear*. What demands ingratitude, hellish negation, parricide, the spike inverted in order to be plunged into the flesh that gave it birth? What produces all that Lear's troubled mind now perceives, which before, in a state of "health," he did not suspect: the startling of the womb, the inferno looming in a woman's genitals, the double edge of lust and sin?

Nietzsche, speaking about Oedipus, remembers a very ancient Persian belief: a very wise magus, he says, cannot be born except as the fruit of incest. "We realize thus why the prophetic and dark powers breaking the magic spell which separates the present from the future, severing the rigid law which differentiates, and dispelling the magic of the natural world, must have from the beginning some miraculous unnaturalness — incest in this case — as their cause." This comment is intriguing, but we should ask whether incest conceals something deeper, inexpressible. Does it convey in the language of the myth a bloodstained riddle, grafted to the very root of life? "We all come from such marriages," says Mrs. Alving, at an illuminating moment in Ibsen's *Ghosts*, bringing the question down to the social level. But something is hidden here that greatly transcends the social; something sinful, long before the sin against authority.

The plague of Thebes has dimensions in depth, as well as in breadth. Its results are dreadful, especially because these results and the mourning of the city reveal the will of a god. A god who strikes with thunder. Sophocles must have retained vividly the image Homer gives us in the *Iliad*: Apollo descending like the night, standing far off and shooting his arrows continually for nine days and nights into the camp of the Achaeans so that the plague would occur:

> *He descended like the night.*
> *He sat down far from the ships and shot an arrow;*
> *dreadful was the din from his silver bow.*
>
> (I, 47–49)

Creon's question, after his return from Delphi, whether Oedipus wishes to go inside with him to announce the prophecy, makes for one of the first clouds. It implies not merely something secret and unpropitious, but something entirely ill-omened and threatening. What is intensified here, even more than the spectator's curiosity, is his anguish, the first consequence of awe. The religiousness of the general atmosphere is heightened by the entrance of Creon, a person who at other times is so worldly. Behind the characters, their encounters, relations, situations, an invisible web has begun to be woven, which comprises the play's essential plot and meaning. As the perceptible action advances, the more tightly this web will be woven and entangled, making perceptible to us something like the hidden plan of a god.

Oedipus Tyrannus' action therefore unfolds on two levels: the perceptible and the spiritual. One sheds light upon the other. Likewise, from their close correlation, from their tangency, arise the most difficult problems ever posed to reason by the tragic genre. The most familiar problem refers to the hero's free will. If *Oedipus Tyrannus* provides us with the model of the tragedy of fate, then tragedy is also the triumphant refutation of responsibility. After this, only by a singularly perfidious and treacherous manipulation could one maintain, resorting to sophistries, that tragedy is the poem of dramatic freedom. Instead, it must also be the representation of ultimate ruin . . .

We have arrived at the central problem of the tragic genre. It should not be considered an evasion if we put it off. It is necessary to clarify our way first.

Sophocles is not a dramatic poet who indulges in meanderings and circumlocutions to arouse the spectator's curiosity with devices. His method is precisely the opposite: a vertical and direct thrust into his theme. Already in his third reply Creon states boldly:

> *Clearly, Lord Phoebus commands us*
> *to drive away the miasma this land*
> *nourishes . . .*
>
> (96–98)

The strong word here is *miasma*. What had cast its shadow over Cadmus' city is irrelevant to fate, eccentricity, or even the god's wrath. Beyond the plague, the calamity of Thebes is due to the *miasma*. Something sacred and in-

violable has been profaned, the disturbance released by
the drama is deeper than a conflict, or a moral dispute.
The whole play will be constructed upon the concept of
the *miasma.*

And immediately from Oedipus' mouth will be uttered
the corresponding religious term: "Through what purification?" (99).

From here the two men, Oedipus and Creon, communicate on this plane; they have transferred the question
there, without any delay. I do not want to call this plane
"metaphysical" because the term has been slandered; it
reminds one of generalities and irresponsibilities. In
Oedipus Tyrannus, on the contrary, as in *Hamlet,* and
Macbeth, the conflict takes place on the most concrete
and crude worldly plane. The shadows projected upon
the mental screen are alluding precisely to something suggestive of a different dimension. If we spoke of metaphysics, therefore, we would have done something improper:
we would have transferred the center of gravity to the
imperceptible, which does not exist except as a foundation upon which the perceptible is projected.

Our search begins haphazardly and simply, with a sequence of questions and answers in reply to a plausible
question: "What is this *miasma?*" "The murderers of King
Laius." "And where could they be after so many years?"
"In this land, here, says the god." Main and secondary
questions accumulate, raise rapidly the temperature until
a question is asked which at once entails a crucial element:

> OEDIPUS: *What misfortune prevented you when
> your king has fallen thus, from
> investigating this?*
>
> (128–129)

A natural question. The response seems no less natural:

CREON: *That enchanting songstress, the Sphinx.*

(130)

The Sphinx had made an apt maneuver. Until now we knew her to be somehow loosely, episodically related to Oedipus and his life. Installed at the entrance of the city, she had posed her riddle to every passerby. Oedipus arrives there too, one day, stops, gives an answer, etc. But with the explanation Creon has just provided, another role of the Sphinx is revealed: Not only had she inaugurated Oedipus' ascent to the throne and his incest, but she also had prevented the timely search for the truth. If Laius' murderers had been sought immediately, perhaps none of this would have happened. But Oedipus was trapped by the Sphinx. There is a secret inner relation between the monster of Boeotia and the oracle of Delphi. It is not something accidental. On this plane of unutterable economy, we have no right to consider anything as accidental. Oracle and Sphinx appear as though serving the same hidden design. The former prophesies what the latter will carry out, and the latter will abet the fulfillment of the oracle in future time in the cruelest possible way.

What in all this is the will of the unknown that we call the divine?

We have arrived by a different path at the same question asked of us earlier in a somewhat different form. A secret plan shapes Oedipus' life, and whatever this economy may intimate, sacred or infernal, the hero seems trapped from birth. No matter what road we take, we see the same question appearing before us irrevocably, relentlessly. Sooner or later, it will be necessary to give an answer. An answer, of course, must also have been given by the poet; otherwise he would not have written the play. Is *Oedipus Tyrannus* an answer to the most crucial question of dramaturgy? No, it is not! It poses the most crucial question of life. Hence its profound significance.

Let us generalize then: Either in an explicit, eloquent way, as the poetics of the myth simplifies it, or in a secret, inexplicable way; one way or another, we seem condemned to pass through the Clashing Rocks, determining both our course and its various changes. This is what we call life: passing through the Clashing Rocks. What more remains? What in order to establish a self-sufficiency intrinsic to our character? And, in the language of our times: are we free perhaps because each time we make a choice, our freedom consists in the facileness of a black or a white ballot, or are we slaves of an annihilating determinism, binding us both from within and without? Are we free perhaps because this is only myth, deceptive idols, figments of the imagination, and we have been cast unprotected, ungoverned, into the midst of a universe without plan, law, order, purpose, hierarchy, or system of values?

Before we try to give an answer — if, presumably, we have the boldness to give one — it is imperative to examine the poet's answer. It is he whom we are interpreting, or, more precisely, it is his thought we are trying to diagnose, for he belongs to the lawmakers of tragedy. For the moment, we acknowledge as tragedy what Sophocles intuited and divined.

But he has given us his first answer already: the feeling that creates the atmosphere of the play's opening, its general climate. This suggests, as we have seen, a holiness. Everything alludes to something, leads to something, gives forth something. The incense fumes winding slowly, le-

thally, despairingly, through the atmosphere of *Oedipus*
are not for decorum: they bear witness to something. A
sense that something sublime is diffused everywhere, determines life and the world. This is what the play will try
to decipher. *Oedipus Tyrannus* is an exploration in the
realm of the inexplorable.

How does it attempt it? Through certain questions that
it poses, the hardest questions. The hardest possible way.
The play chooses the most difficult path, for it is the only
one that can lead to awareness. What meaning is there
in a world where we see an eminent man coming to grips
with the inevitable? Is this man eminent because an unbearable lot has befallen him? Is he eminent *and yet*
persecuted? And, perhaps, is his own lot truly exceptional,
or may it symbolize, in an extreme, mythological language,
Man's fate? With these questions, which do nothing more
than analyze the play's givens, we see that the drama of
Laius' son is played out under a firmament full of complex
symbols, where the light is fire.

Even with the risk of lapsing into monotony, we cannot
neglect the immediately ensuing elements which solidify
and condense the play's metaphysical (the term here is
inevitable) atmosphere. The entrance of the Chorus especially, with its characteristically exalted parodos: "O
sweetly spoken voice of Zeus . . ." (151). I feel it is necessary at this point to repeat that ancient religions, despite
their purely anthropomorphic, and at times childlike innocent representation, despite their mythological biogra-
phies, are less tangible than the Christian belief. Not so
much because they symbolize natural forces and conditions in a composite way, but because they lack a theology:
the theoretical armor forming a closed, formidable, logi-

cally complete system, a given religious belief. Proof of
this is that these deities found themselves defenseless even
against the first questions — let alone disputations — of
ancient philosophy. The thought of Greek philosophers
developed at the unguarded frontiers of religion, or after
this thought had itself dissolved religion into thin air, just
as the wind dissolves a gilded cloud at sunset. The suc-
cessive deities invoked by the Chorus at the parados (O
Zeus ... Delian Paean ... immortal Athena ... Artemis ...
Phoebus . . . Bacchus . . .) refract the meaning of the divine
into a number of forces, helpful or irrelevant. In the midst
of the storm that batters the city, there is a real rainbow
with iridescent colors, glowing profusely over the setting
of the drama. The enumeration of the gods, the way it
occurs and the lyrical radiance of each, broadens the meaning of the divine, diffuses it over all creation, a creation
standing silent but vigilant. The pantheistic spirit, in its
most radiant manifestation, enlivens the domain of the
drama.

After the parados, I want to call attention to Oedipus'
proclamation, which follows right after it. The proclamation is not limited to heightening, in an absolute way, the
dramatic intensity that has already charged the situation.
It introduces an element which elucidates and makes
palpable the religious authority of the leader. The pro-
scription of Laius' murderer is phrased in purely ritualistic
language laden with analogous meaning. It is the proclamation of an anathema from the holy tribune:

> I proclaim that no one should welcome this man,
> whoever he may be, here, in this land where I rule
> and have my throne, or speak to him,
> or give him a share in the prayers and sacrifices to the gods,
> or offer him sacred water to wash his hands;

> *but all should drive him away from their homes,*
> *for he is the miasma, as the Pythian god's oracle*
> *has just revealed to me.*
>
> (236–243)

This anathema has a double quality: Oedipus delivers the curse both as family leader and as religious leader.

> *And for those who will not obey, I pray to the gods*
> *that the fields they plough will bear no crops,*
> *their women no children, but perish*
> *by the same, or even worse, death.*
>
> (269–272)

In spite of what Bernard Knox has said, *Oedipus Tyrannus* originates in patriarchal times. That which connects it with the fifth-century way of thinking, its tempo, is morphological, as is the case always with every literary work, which cannot fail to bear the seal of its times. But the poet, in order to write the tragedy, elevated himself to a dimension requiring a space that was not historically contemporaneous, a wider, deeper one with a mythical foundation. Similarly, in order to search for the metaphysical, the poet plunges himself into his innermost soul, forgetting the prosaic circumlocutions of his contemporary sophists, so as to envision the climate, the situations, and the characters of his play. Ancient drama, with the exception of a certain aspect of Euripides, is an ascent to magnitudes beyond everyday life. I stress this point because I believe it to be one of the constituents of tragedy, irrelevant to temporal qualifications. Just as the tragic heroes transcend common stature, the mediocrity of everyday experience, so the air they breathe is different from that of the marketplace.

With Teiresias' entrance, the god nearly manifests his appearance in person.

OEDIPUS: *O Teiresias, judge of all things,*
            the known and the ineffable, the heavenly
            and the earthly . . .

                                        (300–301)

It is the royal gate, through which the "unbuilt light" will enter to initiate the revelation. At the head is the divine wisdom; it will shortly be followed by the human testimony that verifies it — but too late. Tragedy is inscribed within this frame of badly gauged time. Here tragedy appears to mean poor — and therefore ruinous — estimation of values.

Teiresias' presence on stage makes the question of Apollo shine brightly and dominate. From this point on, the Athenian spectator knew that the drama would unravel under the star of the god of Delphi. The troupe of the other gods who were evoked in the parodos has passed by, is gone. Only Apollo's luminous shadow remains behind to be projected over the play. And it is ominous.

Our tendency toward simplification, particularly of concepts which no longer have any value for our contemporary world, but which constitute a typical knowledge, makes us see in Apollo a serene and radiant god, plastically beautiful, a lawmaker of harmony, the incarnation of pure reason, the quintessential "Hellenic" god. Nietzsche, who distinguished him as an idea in order to juxtapose him to Dionysus, is perhaps responsible for this formulation. In reality, Apollo is an awesome god.

According to myth, Leto, Apollo's mother, when she was about to give birth to him, wandered driven here and there, unable to find a place to stop and give birth, for everyone was afraid of the dreadful god who would come to light. This myth alone is enough to give us a hint of what is concealed behind the symbol. Apollo's identification with the sun, the marvelous and relentless light of a meridional country, speaks eloquently. This god sends forth a radiance that strikes like thunder. Apollo and Artemis, brother and sister, are often mentioned as gods of death — even here we see the concept of light acquiring another, metaphysical significance. There is a light which, when it illuminates you, kills you. An unbearable light. Could the etymology of Apollo's name be derived from the word apollunai (destroy), indicating the ruinous power of this deity? It is enough to recall Cassandra's dreadful madness in *Agamemnon*, when she is seized by her prophetic frenzy:

> *Apollo, Apollo*
> *my Leader, and my destroyer.*
> *You have destroyed me completely this second time.*
> (1080 1082)

The god's presence in the royal slave, in this vessel of his choice, ruins, leads to madness. It is this god Electra invokes at the dreadful moment of matricide in Sophocles:

> *Lord Apollo, hear them propitiously*
> . . . .
> *But now, O Lycean Apollo, I beg*
> *with what I have, I fall prostrate, I entreat,*
> *be our eager helper in these thoughts . . .*
> (1376–1381)

The influence of the Delphic god, however, is never criminal, in the sense of being unjust. It is a punishing and relentless influence. Apollo, giver of the moral law, demands for expiation not the blood of the murderer, as do the primitive Furies, but purification. Only often the sacrifice of blood is included in this purification. Purification is a formidable demand. Someone must pay for it.

Apollo is also the god of prophecy, knows the things of the future, sees afar, foresees. The frenzy that possesses his hierophants, whether Pythia or Sibyl or Cassandra, suggests a transference into another state of mind, an ecstatic exaltation, which is the crossing of the border between the life of ordinary experience and the illumination of the hierophants. Thus we have, at the very center of the Greek world, evidence of the existence of another truth, beyond the one available to everyone, and which, whether or not it represents an intuition or a lofty nostalgia, remains one of the most profound confessions of the ancient soul.

Finally, in order to understand the concept, or rather the system of concepts and experience concealed under the name of Apollo, it is necessary to free ourselves once and for all from the representation of the facetious, ridiculed Twelve Gods, as they have superfically come down to us. A god always takes on the quality of the individual who utters his name. In every period, man has personified under various names of deities the same concept of the ineffable, the holy Unknown. The divine, in the conscience of a poet like Sophocles, can be — and is — an incomparably loftier experience than in the conscience of a foolish worshiper-of-forms or a selfish Christian. When, therefore, we come across the name Apollo in *Oedipus Tyrannus,* let us forget the childish concept of the Twelve Gods, which is a folk superstition of those times, and listen to the great voice speaking to us across thousands of years about the most dreadful presence man has ever felt at his side.

We are not attempting a methodical analysis of the play, we are only following some veins of precious metal ramified through it; that is why the sequence of our thoughts does not correlate with the drama's development.

From the long scene between Oedipus and Teiresias — one of the gems of poetic drama both in content and in progression — I will mention one line only. It is the well-known epigrammatic line of Teiresias: "This day will give you birth and ruin you" (438).

It would be a commonplace to say that this line contains the play's meaning. But some commonplaces are obligatory: they lead to something beyond. This one leads to the heart of a riddle much more difficult than the riddle of the Sphinx: Why is the play's hero destroyed the way he is destroyed?

A great deal has been said. Oedipus is punished, they say, because he committed unlawful acts: he killed his father and slept with his mother ("But he did not know it." "It doesn't matter!"). Oedipus is punished because he committed a "hubris." Oedipus is punished because he is irritable, autocratic, proud. These answers depend on a more or less classroom mentality. If a person suffered such terrible things, he must have been in the wrong. And the established art of drama does not believe in anything different. Can a punishment be conceived without culpability? Of course, a small problem remains: the disproportion between the wrong and the punishment. It is overwhelming. But classroom morality, when referring to classical texts, bypasses such issues lightheartedly or writes them off to tragic economy: It would be a pity if dreadful and wretched things did not happen in a tragedy! Where else should they happen?

However, we see a suspicious flickering. Teiresias' line and the play's riddle seem to lead into a morality unexpected by those of us who subscribe to a one-dimensional concept of morality. Something tells us that under this disproportion is hidden perhaps the most profound secret of the tragic genre, or even something awesome in itself. That is why I proposed *Oedipus Tyrannus* for our first example.

As Teiresias says during the crisis of the play, Oedipus is bound to "be born" today. This is the play's target as well: a man will be brought into the light. Birth, we are told, is a mystery; and we are now called upon to witness it. But the mystery in Teiresias' line, they will explain, has a double meaning: to be born means to open our eyes to a hidden truth. The question is what these eyes, which will in any case lose their light immediately, forever, will open on — on the hero's past, his origin? On his errors? On his life's riddle, which remains unsolved? Or on the mysterious will of the gods? Teiresias speaks like an oracle; he suggests, he does not reveal or exhaust the meaning. But for precisely this reason the margin of interpretation appears broader to our eyes. Together with the hero, it will also be necessary for us to recover our sight. One cannot be fulfilled without the other. Otherwise, Oedipus' drama will remain inexplicable and unjustified . . .

It is not accidental that the disproportion of *Dike* (Justice) and *hamartia* remains inexplicable in *Oedipus Tyrannus.*

At this point, I would like to ask a simple, even a naïve, question: in reading the play, or in seeing it performed, do we perhaps form the impression that the hero is suffering unjustly? This is of primary significance, because if Oedipus is indeed suffering unjustly, then instead of a drama we have a scandal and our reaction to it suits the predicament of someone who is "defiled," according to Aristotle. We should be careful, though, not to mistake our emotion — pity and fear — because it is intense, for our psychic disturbance vis-à-vis an unjustly suffering man. It is one thing to witness the execution of hostages, and another to see Oedipus without eyes. We shudder, shrink, feel compassion for him, we secretly feel that he is not at all alien to us, despite the odd nature of his story; yet, we do not revolt against his ruthless destiny. Do we think he deserves this destiny? That is another question. I believe that in this inconceivable distance between what ought to have happened and what actually did happen lies the metaphysics of tragedy.

We term Oedipus' suffering disproportionate and accept it, but not out of blind fortitude. We recognize in it a reality of life, part of an unwritten and entirely ruthless law of the world. Of *this* world, into which, one day, we discover that we are sent to live without having been asked. This means that it is futile to judge the rules of the game. Whether we accept or disapprove of them, we have to play the game, we have to live by its rules, for no other rules exist or are suitable. And our role, the assertion of our self, remains confined to a marginal endeavor: to guess, if we can, what is hiding behind these inherent laws. We cannot. But neither do we desist. We make an effort to see whether it will be possible from the inherent structure of the law, from its overall appearance, from its physiognomy, to surmise the form which the Lawmaker may take.

Why is this necessary? Not to satisfy our curiosity. Not to expiate ourselves or associate ourselves with Supreme Authority. There is a more passionate reason: to see whether the adventure is worthwhile, whether it corresponds to something that justifies it, to something that gives an answer — indirect, meager, even — to our claim for dignity. Are we perhaps negligible quantities, playthings in the hands of the gods, or do we express a unique quality? In granting us self-consciousness, have they deceived us?

Tragedy now becomes an endeavor to lay the foundations for a dignity in this world, *before* God reveals himself. An endeavor *because* God continues to remain silent. In this lies its *human* nature. It is an attempt for man to find his own law within himself. It should be noted that this concerns an aesthetic not a moral law. Moral law requires a fellow player, a response, a reference to a system of values, an objective or transcendent sanction. Aesthetic law is self-sufficient; it has only one judge: man. Hence the disparity we meet in tragedy between moral claim and aesthetic affirmation.

But ill-mannered as we are from the routine of everyday life, we try to transfer its economy to the realm of tragedy. And it is here that spuriousness begins. We say: "Why did Orestes have to commit matricide? What moral can be derived from such a paradigm?" And furthermore: "What kind of god allows such things — and even more, imposes them? What does he mean to reveal?" But such language has no place here. The paradox of tragedy lies in the fact that though it raises the question with all its being, it has supplied an irrelevant answer. It is a self-reliant answer, like aesthetic law, which constitutes a value in and of itself. We must be cautious! The answer does not abolish the question. The question remains persistent, relentless. There exists a reckoning of tragedy with itself, the outcome of which is aesthetic, and also a reckoning of tragedy with the divine. In the latter, silence is metaphysical. In tragedy's economy we find an extreme, perilous balance between an outcome and a silence. The silence magnifies the outcome and the outcome magnifies the silence.

To "be born" in Teiresias' language (we shall discover this along with Oedipus, in the end) means not only to enlighten oneself, to learn, to be taught a lesson and find one's sight; above all it means "to exist." To the hero's question, What mortal man has given him birth? the harsh seer replies: "hed' hemera" ("this very day") (438). It is not a "brotos" ("mortal") (437) who has given you birth, but a day, a link in time's correlation, a restless, bright link, which will culminate in life's suffering. Before this day, you did not exist. You were insubstantial, a wandering shadow, prey to fortune, though you envisioned yourself as "megan" ("great") (441). You were without parentage, citizenship, identity. You were a bastard, because those whom you called your parents were strangers. Sunken into absolute deception, you, the solver of riddles, were proud of your keenness of mind. You, the victor over the Sphinx, have become her unsuspecting victim. How can a person, groping, become a human being, become conscious in darkness? Thus, even before you recover your sight, you must come into the light. This is what Oedipus' birth may have been. And his birth might also have meant his ruin. The hero will perish *because* he came into the light. We have said there is a light that destroys.

Is it perhaps the light of truth in the sense of a conscious contact with reality? In other words, is it knowledge and awareness? The reference to Apollo warns us this is not so. Without it being stated explicitly, and *exactly because it is not stated explicitly*, we perceive from the context that the light which will strike Oedipus at a certain moment and annihilate him is a different kind of light. The play's revelation does not depend on a warning (ultimately, Oedipus learns who his parents were). That terrifying line of his at the end, "It was Apollo, Apollo, my friends" (1329), is a semi-conscious, semi-unconscious pronouncement, like all inner illuminations. The Delphic "hekabolos" ("far-shooting") god flung his flame from afar and scorched him. We have witnessed a horrid mystery which foreshadows the hero's end in *Oedipus at Colonus*.

But what value may there be in the illumination that comes to a person who is alienated by definition, the captive of an irrevocable preordination? And what may this illumination mean? This is what remains for us to examine.

IV

The Impure Root and
the Perfectly Pure Light–II

THE LOGICAL and metaphysical scandal in *Oedipus Tyrannus* rests in its three oracles: this tangle of prophecies and pronouncements closing in on the hero's life and molding it into *moira* (fate). This remains clear, whether Sophocles projects it according to the model of the original myth or not. The Athenian spectator knows it and the poet has done nothing to eliminate or restrain it. On the contrary, we are reminded of it by the main characters at critical points in the play. Jocasta relates the oracle concerning Laius; Oedipus tells his own oracle; Creon tells the oracle to the city. The first said, "You will be killed by the son you will beget." The second: "You will become the husband of your mother, you will sow an unholy race and kill your father." The third: "The *miasma* must be expelled from the city because the evil will become incurable."

This is the historical order of the oracles. In the play, we learn first of the third oracle, then the first, and finally the second. The inversion is not accidental. It is dictated by dramatic recurrence. The mystery reaches a climax so as to gather the force needed to unveil itself. The climax is also dictated by another more important factor: the need to evoke in us the play's secret nature. God is not revealed suddenly; he removes the veils one by one. Thus, the mystery that aimed at suspense becomes a mystery evoking awe.

This impression is supported by the innate differences in the oracles. Of the three, only the first two are prophecies. The third demands a purgation.

Those who stress the play's structure unconsciously underline the importance of suspense, whereas the play's essence, its raison d'être, is awe. *Oedipus Tyrannus,* like all great plays, functions by suggestion. Without abandoning even momentarily the earth's warm ground, it constantly allows something else to be implied, projected upon an invisible screen far off in the background. Tragedy, anyway, is always played on two levels: one perceptible, the other imperceptible.

In no other play has the dreadful question of predestination been presented with such clarity, acuteness, or in such mythological, epigrammatic form, as in *Oedipus Tyrannus.* One realizes immediately that the poet has confronted it as a challenge. He may well have chosen Oedipus' myth for precisely this reason: to provide his own interpretation of the problem. Otherwise, there was no reason to write an *Oedipus* after Aeschylus. But even if he chose this subject from purely artistic inspiration, he again reached the same conclusion. The fatal concurrence of events that shapes the life of Laius' son was a challenge precisely within the value system of an Athenian tragic poet.

Penelope Gilliat, reviewing a 1965 joint presentation of *Oedipus Tyrannus* and *Oedipus at Colonus* in the *London*

Observer, suggests that it is a commonplace to say that Greek drama is remote from us because of its causal character. To be more specific: a man who believes his life can be destroyed because of the curse of the gods does not appear tragic to us; he appears as a disparagement. The only kind of causality we may generally accept today, and this unwillingly, is not the supernatural but the psychological: an inevitability that arises not from oracles but from personal traits. This is, in fact, the first impression of the play's structure. Indeed, so much so that one wonders, as one weighs one's impressions, how we are left with the feeling of an authentic tragedy and with the impression of absolute tragic dignity in specific regard to the hero and heroine. Has Sophocles succeeded then, with his refined art, in maintaining this difficult and deceptive balance? Has he skillfully averted our attention and concealed the problem? Or — and perhaps this is a question we ask prematurely — can a deeper secret of tragedy be hidden here?

First, in chronological order and significance, comes the oracle to Laius. What gives it special dramatic gravity is the way in which Jocasta announces it. Her intention is to calm Oedipus. Thus the content of the most significant tragic irony is revealed. It is our duty to draw certain conclusions from it, because if the words are Jocasta's, and they are placed at this point in the drama and not at any other, then they must actually be the poet's. By employing tragic irony, Sophocles wished to suggest Jocasta's deception, hence the decisive and immutable gravity of the oracle. The heroine's entire speech is written with exquisite craftsmanship in nuances:

No mortal possesses the art of prophecy.
. . . .

An oracle was told to Laius once, I do not say
from Phoebus himself, but from his priests

. . . .

And here Apollo did not allow him
to become his father's killer, nor Laius
to die by his son's hand as he feared.

. . . .

. . . the things God deems
necessary to explore, he will himself easily reveal.

(709–725)

At what does the god's acquittal aim? An acquittal refuted by what follows? Or is it perhaps a touch of Jocasta's
character, showing her as god-fearing in spite of what she
will say later at moments of obstinate hope or triumphant
oratory? Is it an indirect indictment and not an acquittal
of the god who is shown as strange, incomprehensible, and
mocking of men's hopes? Is it a stressing of a metaphysical
disparity between human intelligence and divine will and
economy?

The hero's sudden outburst sheds some light here:

Just as I was listening to you, O woman,
what turmoil of soul and stirring of mind seized me.

(726–727)

O Zeus, what are you planning for me in your mind?

(738)

For the first time, the god's ax flashed overhead, and
Oedipus, chilled by its cold radiance, felt it. A willful deception then, Jocasta's words were a belated flattery to the
god. This woman, though in her consciousness innocent,
is burdened with a crime. She is her son's wife, she who

once unprotestingly gave her infant to be thrown to the wild beasts of Cithaeron. For the second time, though to a lesser degree, the problem of guilt or rather of *miasma* appears here. Just as the son, to a greater degree, will be shown to be defiled with his father's blood and his mother's embrace, so the mother is burdened with complicity in her child's murder and in incest. Objectively speaking, ignorance does not make the unholy act less dreadful. Incest, in particular, appears to be one of the first prohibitions at the base of a civilized society; the anathema linked to it has settled in the depths of collective memory. For the ancient metaphysical conscience, defilement is always defilement, something like a hereditary stigma that must be cleansed. One may feel pity for the defiled person, but this makes him no less repugnant. There is something here like a foretaste of original sin, only it does not concern mankind, but certain tragic individuals. In the presence of the divine, man very early on felt impure, sinful, because very early he became conscious of his limitations and moral weaknesses. One way of expressing reverence toward the Supreme Authority is the humility of accepting the responsibility for one's sinful existence. One way of acknowledging man's weakness is to perceive that we constantly live side by side with sin. But even beyond this, guilt in being constitutes *the supreme tragic intuition.*

We should mention two more recent encounters with the question. "Every happy man is guilty," wrote Charles Péguy about *Oedipus Tyrannus.* And Jean Marie Domenach, who mentions Péguy's dictum in his essay "The Return of the Tragic" (1927), expands this view: "The tragic therefore appears from the beginning as a premonition of a guilt without concrete cause, the self-evidence of which is almost beyond dispute." In essence, Hegel did not see the problem differently in the dialectics of Christian thought: the ascetic torments himself to prove that the body is worthy of contempt; but he does not kill it. He allows it just as much life as it needs to continue its suffering. But the body revolts because it is tormented, and the more it revolts, the more the ascetic torments it. Whence an enormous feeling of guilt in the soul of the ascetic. "He must necessarily feel guilty, and in fact guilty without hope of salvation, to justify this endless condemnation," writes André Aman, summing up Hegel's view in his very important book *Europe Made the World*. "This mystery of a guilt that burdens innocence," writes Domenach again, "cannot be understood in a purely rational way. The task of tragedy is to represent it, that of philosophy to dispute it. This dialectic marks out the history of tragedy, its zenith and its prolonged eclipses ... Undoubtedly Oedipus' irrational guilt refers to some beginning which has become indecipherable for us, and to which the Greeks could still get close." In the above encounters, the feeling of guilt acquires a strange flexibility. It appears to emanate from some immemorial source, beyond pure reason; it is formulated in mythological language, like an archetype; it is restricted to the concrete plane of the psychological in the dialectics of the Christian spirit. The feeling of guilt reappears in the divine transformed into a demand, indictment, and thirst for expiation. In simpler words we would say that this original guilt is the only reason man has been able to find for the lifelong expiation of the punishment his life appears to be.

We touch thus upon one of the central questions in *Oedipus*. Mortal man comes into this world not as an isolated incident but endowed with a life history, because he is rooted in Time. His existence is the continuation of man's diachronic existence. Assets and liabilities accompany him. His character, the "ethos" which Heracleitus calls the fate of everyone of us ("Character is destiny for man") is the product of ancestral roots. Just as we cannot rid ourselves of the liabilities of our character, so we cannot rid ourselves of the liabilities of those who have delineated its basic framework. Our blood is borrowed and transmittable. In this causality? Only insofar as it is dictated by Nature, that inexplorable and impersonal legislation we find when we come into this world. Between one's initial ancestral diagram and one's completed life falls the initiative one develops. What is yours? What is not yours? And who are you? It is impossible to answer precisely. The lifelong becoming that man represents quivers at a shadowy border, expresses an enigma, and our sense of responsibility is nothing more than a deceptive façade. Ancient man, with his basic tragic conscience, is aware of this mystery; he does not try artificially or optimistically for a typical or extemporaneous solution. The psychological causality that the contemporary spirit accepts (as the English critic remarks) contains the metaphysical causality, implies it, but does not have the courage to become conscious of it and express it.

But again this interpretation is a transitory one.

Let us get closer to the specific problem. From the play's content we form the following impression: The god had once prophesied to Laius that he would be killed by the son he would have with Jocasta. Laius either did not worry enough or was misled; he had a son. Suddenly, he remembered the oracle and, to save himself, tied the feet of the newly born, and had him taken away to be exposed on the mountain. There are two resulting possibilities: either the god was fooled, or Laius was wrong. The other two oracles are secondary and should not obscure the initial point from us.

Laius, if we believe in the later formulation of the oracle extant in the manuscript of Euripides' *Phoenician Women*, had been condemned by Zeus because he was the first man to come into conflict with the natural order; that is, he fell in love with and eloped with Pelops' young son, Chrysippus. These facts were known to the Athenian spectator. But Sophocles does not want them; he leaves them outside the design of his play. He does not want to give his drama the meaning of an ancestral sin. *He does not want his Oedipus to be condemned for an ancestral sin.*

The god, here, foretells; he does not condemn. What was first noticed by Williamovitz means, very simply, that divine wisdom does not exist. Let us remember this simple thought; we will need it in the end. From the moment the god has prophesied, there are again two alternatives: Either man can rebuff the oracle — but then what kind of oracle can be rebuffed? This is not merely impiety, but pure absurdity. Or the oracle will come true in one way or another, no matter what man does, and then we begin to sense within us the feeling of a condemnation that is not ancestral. But why? Are we perhaps the victims of an inverted order? Let us bring the question onto an everyday plane.

As long as I act in life in a natural way, without knowing exactly what I will do tomorrow, I am certain that I make use of a self-evident privilege: free will. But, let us suppose some person who is antagonistic to me, and who believes in the truth of prophecies, goes for advice to a fortuneteller. She tells what I am going to do in a certain situation. If the prophecy comes true, I have not the slightest doubt that what I did, I did freely. Therefore, I bear the responsibility of the initiative.

Let us suppose now that the person who consults the fortuneteller is my friend. Learning the bad news, he comes and tells me, to protect me. Less credulous than he, I ignore it; I follow a course of action according to my judgment, and — miraculously! — I prove the prophecy true. I had simply disregarded it. What has changed? Why in the first case could we not speak of "condemnation" and in the second case think we can? Yet, again, it is not at all certain that everyone will consider me irresponsible. At most, they will call me unwise, because, though warned, I did not heed, for better or worse.

But there is also a third possibility: the fortuneteller foresees; I am informed. I become anxious, I do everything I can to escape, but I do not succeed. The prophecy comes true in spite of my efforts. What are the terms that have changed here? A single one only: my conduct. A decisive factor, surely, because it reveals free will: it shows whether it is fictitious or real. It is as if a third force had intervened, more powerful than my will, compelling me to do what the fortuneteller had prophesied. *I have acted again, but I did something that appears as if I had not wanted to.*

Does this mean perhaps that the initiative has now transferred to the unknown force that enlightened the fortuneteller? Do we have any other sign for the intervention of this authority outside the prophecy? Or perhaps the unknown force simply *knew* what I would have done anyway in any circumstances. If it is truly a higher force, it should have known it. In conclusion, since it wanted me to do what I did, I must be able to attribute to it an evil intention. But is this not more daring than the acceptance of omniscience? Am I not perhaps the secret destiny of my self, and from a justified human error do I see objectified, mythologized, this necessity of mine? I live in a world without moral authority, that is certain; I easily believe, then, in something that transcends neutral fortuity. With my tendency to give human form to all things, I create a transcendent power, a dark spirit, hostile to myself. This both saddens and flatters me: my enemy is supernatural.

The god's wisdom, whether he is Apollo or whatever the name of the fortuneteller's master is, consists in a knowledge that transcends me, reaches beyond my knowledge. My own acts are within me; an equal number of possibilities. My destiny is my reflection. Prediction is one thing, and predestination another. God predicts what will happen because *I* will do it. God knows me, and he cannot be wrong because he is a god; and I also do not change because I am myself, I have an identity, a life history, an entity. If the fortuneteller, instead of speaking to my friend, had spoken to me, her prediction would be called an oracle. Therefore, it is not the oracle that decides, it is I who decide. The oracle knows. And it knows better than I do, because he who dictated it sees deeper within me than I do. In this lives the wisdom of the god.

Although all this seems obvious we do not intend to make use of practical thoughts alone to refute the concept of indeterminate fate, which, in spite of everything, still remains a vivid impression, although not always the predominant one, in the realm of tragedy. This is not accidental. Tragedy not only does not shun indeterminate

fate but, on the contrary, seeks it. In *Oedipus Tyrannus*
especially, the poet underlines in a thousand ways the preeminence of the god's wisdom, and this means that something fatal is imminent.

From the first stasimon we sense it indirectly, in the
Chorus' distrust of the oracles. It is the most eloquent
possible preparation for the oracles' immediate fulfillment:

> . . . *but whoever says that a seer*
> *understands more than I do,*
> *of that there is no true test;*
> *one man surpasses*
> *another man in wisdom.*
> *I will never assent to accusations*
> *before I know the words are true.*
>
> (499–506)

Here the Chorus appears to be wrong, and it is encouraged in this by its flexible character, its antirealistic in-
consistency, the divine naïveté that makes it into a supple
instrument in the tragic poet's hands. Through the
Chorus, with its fluid attitudes, the drama can be illuminated from different angles, directly or indirectly, boldly,
ironically, or obliquely. Thanks to the Chorus' inconsis
tent utterances, the Aeolian harp brings forth all its harmonies, down to the deepest, most secret ones.

The ancient poet, confronted with the enigma of human
life, and with a myth in his hand as a model, wonders in
anguish. There is something fatal in our development, it
seems, something preordained, regardless of whether it is
perceived within man or elsewhere, inside or outside the
universe. In the life of some people fatality becomes especially discernible and then tragedy begins to be imper-

ceptibly delineated. But the existence of the marked man is fundamentally no different from that of other men. It is only less fortunate, its development is more vulnerable. Thus, from within the whole, some persons with an ill-fortuned privilege stand out, marked on the forehead, and make perceptible to others the fate of humankind. This is their peculiar mission. There exists therefore *a destiny of mankind*, not an antinomic destiny of this or that tragically chosen person.

> *Alas, generations of mortals,*
> *I count your life*
> *as equal to zero.*
> . . . .
> *Having seen your misfortune,*
> *and your destiny,*
> *O unlucky Oedipus, no mortal man*
> *do I call fortunate.*
>
> (1186–1196)

The poet laments for all of us, without exception, along with his hero. Oedipus is a "paradigm," not an exception. How did it happen that this person with the unheard-of, defiled history has been elevated to a paradigm for the whole, a model of humankind? This is not the least of the play's secrets, nor the least important. The oracles that have marked the fate of the son of Laius did not concern him only.

In this light, predestination begins to acquire a different meaning. The fate of the tragic hero is broadened, becomes a symbolically representative case; its strange circumstances have no other purpose than to emphasize the traits of a common fate. In everyday cases, the tragic passes unnoticed. In exceptional cases — that is, in the most elevated — it is both declared and proclaimed. So, if we are to speak of predestination, we ought to extend it to the whole of the human race, to those "generations of mortals" which the Chorus laments in *Oedipus*. Gradually, imperceptibly, the poet has succeeded in involving all of us in the fate of his hero. How did he succeed? What common element did he find in the tragic king of Thebes and in us?

There is no doubt that the world of the tragic is dominated by the feeling that something dark looms in the distant background, something undefined and threatening, inexplicable and unattainable. It cannot take a form like the gods, general ideas, the physical powers. It is impersonal, because it has no characteristics, no history. In its invisible snares, spread like a spider's web, we are all caught, merely because we belong to humankind: our human nature wants it. If we call this dark existence *moira*, then we must first acknowledge that it is not personal but general: not the fate of Orestes or Oedipus but of man, no longer the classical *moira* of the theoreticians of tragedy. And second, that with this word we express nothing concrete. Nothing more concrete than the natural, inherent laws which require that we be born and die, and know that our life has an end; and that we are subject to physical and moral pain, to errors, and to the inescapable; that our brief passing through this world will have the character of a trial, and contain more pain and anguish than joy, pleasure, or carefreeness. Beyond this, whatever else appears seemingly exceptional will be seen, with a little thought, as part of the lot of humankind. *Moira*, therefore, means here what the etymology of the word means: lot, share. It appears here as if tragic fate does not exist as

an exception. Or rather that no other fate exists but tragic
fate.

These thoughts make us realize now that if we are talking of predestination, we ought to perceive it for the whole
of mankind, in a general causality, without exception.
Oedipus' story terrifies us because it stirs within us an undefined fear that is not alien to us. The impurity that lies
in the root of the son of Laius lies at the root of life itself.
This is suggested by the strange feeling of our guilt toward
the divine. It is an impersonal fault, without history, almost, which first hinted at and gave content to the idea
of *hamartia*. They have called Aeschylus the most Jewish
of the ancient tragic poets because he seems to be the first
to conceive the gravity of original sin and founded on it
his entire tragic thought. Every great tragic work, at a certain moment of its being, puts its finger, as if by mistake,
on this dreadful wound. It is the "rotten" in the kingdom
of Denmark in *Hamlet*; it is the world of the chthonic
reversal of principles in *Macbeth*; it is the genetic filth
that the deranged Lear envisions. The ancient drama, less
cynical than the contemporary, lets this condition be suggested, does not denounce it, and, in fact, requires an in-
credible skill on Sophocles' part for us to believe, beyond
a certain point, as his play advances, that we are not
strangers to the blood that defiles Oedipus in the course
of his life: blood of parricide, blood of incest, blood of
gouged eyes. "A black rain of blood like hail" (1278–1279).

Eyes and sight especially occupy a very significant place
in this play. There is an entire metaphysics of light in
Oedipus Tyrannus. It reaches a climax in the act which,
rationally, if it had not been established by tradition,
would seem by itself inexplicable: why self-blindness and
not suicide? The hero's first move, in fact, after the revela-

tion, when he rushed inside the palace in madness, was to kill, and then kill himself.

> *He ran madly toward us asking for a lance,*
> *and for his wife, no wife, and where he might find*
> *the double mother-soil of himself and his children.*
>
> (1255–1257)

But the sight of Jocasta makes him suddenly change his mind, without even finding the time to think:

> *... dreadfully groaned the hapless man;*
> *he loosed the hanging noose; and when the unlucky*
> *woman fell to the ground, it was a horrid sight!*
> *He tore away the golden brooches*
> *which held her clothes . . .*
>
> (1265–1269)

The reversal is automatic, blind, dictated by a dark instinct. Jocasta's brooches, torn off suddenly, reveal to him the naked body of the woman who lustily consumed him in her embrace, and had previously brought him to light. "A wife, no wife . . . mother-soil . . ." The compactness is giddying; the woman's double role, her embrace, is contracted into a revealing epigram. In one single line! Oedipus, striking his eyes with Jocasta's brooches, believes — and he says so — that he does it to keep from seeing his sins ever again. But his action is wiser than his tongue, controlled by the mind. Striking his eyes maniacally "many times and not once" (1275), he punishes the instrument of deception. He punishes it with the brooches of the woman who brought him to light. Of the woman who made him king, who brought him to life, to eternity and deception.

Now Teiresias' eyes, the keen-sightedness of the conqueror of the Sphinx, the signs from Apollo — all these concepts and values which during the play's course relate to light, find their restitution. The light, with its various manifestations, flashes across the play, from beginning to end. It is the natural and the irrational light. The light of the mind and the light of the world. The outer and the inner light. The light that illuminates and the light that strikes like a thunderbolt. The antitheses are not always so distinct, so symmetrical; they also have composite sides: a light that both leads you to life and blinds you. The wealth of radiance emanating from *Oedipus Tyrannus* is unimaginable. And when one feels this, when one relates it to the hero's climactic tragic action, right before the naked body of the woman who gave birth to him, then one realizes that in this correlation is hidden one of the most profound messages of the play.

Not extreme antitheses, we said. Because the two sources of light, the outer and the inner, are for the ancient soul neither contradictory nor unrelated, as they are for our world that has been taught to think in the logical forms of physical science. For the ancient conscience, natural light and irrational light make up complementary tones. Proof of this is that they have the same source, the same god: Apollo. There exists, of course — Oedipus' drama demonstrates this — a hierarchy of the two. But there is no distinction between scorned, material light, and holy light glowing in a world other than the earthly. "O pure light" (86) are Electra's first words. And Aeschylus, the most austere in intelligence of the ancient tragic poets, has said with Prometheus' mouth: "O divine ether" (89). For Aeschylus, even the air which contains the light is sacred.

But see that Oedipus, this justifiably tormented man in the brilliance of his mind — recognized by the priests themselves as almost equal to a god due to his acumen, his intellectual superiority — was sunk neck-deep in deception. As long as he had his eyes, he was sailing in darkness. He recovers his sight when he blinds himself. And this is implicit, the most imperceptible irony in all the play, the one heard at the moment of the farewell to happy life: "O light, I see you for the last time now . . ." (1183).

The irrational light, which is, in its purest form, Apollo, has defeated the light of Reason. Here is the play's "epiphany," the god's revelation. The sight of the blind Teiresias proved more overpowering than the clearsightedness of the solver of the riddles. If there is a hubris in *Oedipus Tyrannus*, it consists of this: the hero's self-confidence and pride in his intellectual awareness. A justified self-confidence, because Nature has endowed him with this light so that he can proceed. It is by this light that Oedipus "proved himself great." But it seems that man is accompanied from the moment he is born by an unwritten contract, an assumed responsibility: to agonize and wonder whether there also exists another light beyond the perceptible. It seems as if the essence of his life is contained in a struggle that has been assigned to him at his birth. If he does not sense it, he is lost.

The lesson has depth as well as breadth. It concerns us all, as human beings. By his nature the human being tends to overestimate his intellect, because it is the value that seems to justify him metaphysically and grant him a self-independence in the creation. Fifth-century Athens, the city that set up on pedestals for the first time Reason and

Humanism, tended toward this overestimation of the rational light. Sophocles reminds Athens of this at times. With the triumph of the physical sciences, our present era shares this same tendency, is subject to this same temptation. Every era striving for its own lights is subject to it. The confrontation is noble, worthy of the spirit of tragedy, which knows nothing but justified values, albeit antagonistic ones. As for conflict and catastrophe, if these could be avoided, tragedy would not have a metaphysical root. It would be man's mise-en-scène. A diversion.

There is also a third idea, which the poet has employed to broaden the basis of his play and give it the universality it has. It is crystallized in those elements that project the hero's symbolically human side.

Its loftiest, most spiritual expression is his supreme passion, the one that urges him to search persistently for his identity. On the one hand we see it manifested as an abstract thirst for truth and knowledge; but on the other it is man's specific psychological need to know who he is, what is his origin, who gave him birth. The latter comprises the longing for human and social dignity. The former, the claim which defines mankind ontologically: the restless inquiring spirit.

According to Athenian law, the prosecution of a murderer could not be undertaken ex officio by the city, but only by a relative of the victim. This adds to *Oedipus Tyrannus* a note of latent pathos, unfortunately lost for us today: the prosecution of Laius' murderer will be undertaken by his son, although he does not know it. He will be able to learn it in the end, at the moment he discovers that he was not a *tyrannos*, a usurper of the throne, but its legal successor, therefore a king. Oedipus is proclaimed a king — ultimate irony — at his fall! At this moment he gains legal status. A sinful king. What was it that wanted Oedipus to become a king through guilt?

The theme of the "Priest at Nemi," as Frazer describes it in *The Golden Bough,* echoes here very distantly. Nobody had the right to succeed the priest of Artemis in the Roman groves at Nemi except the man who would kill him. The priestly duty passed from hand to hand by murder: the younger and stronger had to kill his predecessor, just as this one had done before him. Two complementary quotations from Frazer illuminate the picture from an aspect that interests us: "The union of a royal title with priestly duties was common in ancient Italy and Greece." And, "In those days the divinity that hedges a king was no empty form of speech, but the expression of a somber belief. Kings were revered, in many cases not merely as priests, that is, as intercessors between man and god, but as themselves gods, able to bestow upon their subjects and worshippers those blessings which are commonly supposed to be beyond the reach of mortals, and are sought, if at all, only by prayer and sacrifice offered to superhuman and invisible beings."

This ancient myth of the priest at Nemi, with its automatic interrelations, shows us the immemorial depth of Oedipus' myth.

But if the act of parricide transfers the question once again to a mythological plane, other characteristics bring it down to earth, to a purely, incurably, human level: from a royal race but without knowing his origin, an exposed and wounded infant, marked by the sign of pain, of contempt for life; a traveler driven to solve riddles and read oracles in order to proceed; a vagabond with the spark of insatiable curiosity in his eyes, created to sin unwillingly and pay for actions unknown to him — who is this man? Who else but Man?

The Oedipus of the Athenian tragic poet no longer appears so isolated in the nightmare of his life. Behind him journeys the whole human race. The strange footprint of his myth, which till now seemed like a riddle, has suddenly congealed into a family monogram.

V

An Everlasting Death

Ay, we must die an everlasting death.
— Marlowe, *Doctor Faustus*

WE CAN SAY that in *Oedipus Tyrannus* we have a
model of the tragic that accords with the consciousness of the world that first had the privilege to conceive it.
We saw it steeped in the secret light of a religion that
remains hermetically sealed for us today, and only intuitively perceptible. The question that follows now is
whether tragedy is so closely interwoven with the circumstances, the inner climate, the cosmological rhythm, of
that time that it will remain its untransmittable posses-
sion, or whether beneath its initial expression there looms
something permanent, which in each instance finds the
proper way of manifesting itself.

Without digressing, it will be necessary to say that we
are not tracing the tragic generally and vaguely, in life, society, history, or art, but in the theater. This last remark,
though, is redundant: tragedy is a theatrical and only a
theatrical expression. Not in the sense that it concerns

some arbitrary privilege, but because the tragic genre requires for its completion the aesthetic conditions of the
theater: a life of the second degree, with its own beginning,
middle, and end; its own dialectics, presence, rules, necessity, and economy.

If the later world had not rediscovered the course of
the tragic cry, we would say that its first utterance was an
accidental event, unrepeatable, therefore a unique result
of certain historical conditions. We would also lack any
means of perceiving it tangibly as a reality. Tragedy would
not express a man's secret yet permanent suspicion. And
if we saw it being reproduced in exactly the same way, in
its ancient mode, amidst a world so different, we would
show disbelief, and say that it was not a phenomenon
possessing its own strength, but a regurgitation. And this
is what, indeed, happened in the first phase of the renas-
cent world. The historian of the theater who objectively
follows its developments has the duty to record this. Our
duty is to bypass it. Tragedy leads us with its torches
burning through the forest of the Furies. If it were to
usher us onto a stage setting made of paper and wood, better it did not exist. Something tells me that the stage of
tragedy is not a mere raised platform.

We shall stop at a point in the theater that appears to
be the first genuine tragic cry in the Christian world. Perhaps it has something to teach us. It is so early a work
that it remains primitive, unpolished, incomplete, but for
precisely this reason it convinces with its authenticity.
Christopher Marlowe's *Tragic History of Doctor Faustus*
was written, it seems, circa 1588. The only certain dates
for the play are 1600–1601, the first record of the pub-
lisher's copyright, and 1604, its first known edition.

All this is not pointless philological information; it de-

fines a period. The Elizabethan theater, newly awaking
from its medieval torpor, makes at this time its first staggering steps. Only one fourth of *Doctor Faustus* can be
called a play for the theater; the remaining, in its general
external structure, is a Morality, a petty squabble, child-
ishly uneven and medievally rough. It does not matter
whether its author knew — through Seneca maybe — the
existence and, in its general outlines, the structure, of the
classical dramatic play. What matters is his dedication,
conscious or unconscious, to the native forms imposed
upon him by the living tradition. *Doctor Faustus* is not
an imitation. It is an original phenomenon.

But can we also consider it as a new discovery of those
elements that the ancient tragedy had once given us and
which had been forgotten? Does it perhaps add to them?
Is this new phenomenon their transubstantiated expression? Has the later world added anything to the revelation
of the tragic? Something which represents and comple-
ments it? Or has it confined itself to modifying slightly
the initial forms? Has it perhaps found variations which
give breadth and depth to the basic questions?

For the Christian world *Doctor Faustus* is something
like the Book of Job. A cry of metaphysical rebellion, it
is a play that vacillates in full dizziness between blasphemy and contrition. Between ultimate blasphemy and
ultimate contrition. Its relation to the poet's personal life,
a life highly turbulent, inconsistent, and cut short in
its thirtieth year, is not anecdotal. About Marlowe we
know just enough to obscure his personality. Did he believe or was he an atheist? Had he decided between the
two? Is the position he takes in *Doctor Faustus* totally
confessional or does he adapt it externally to the moral
restrictions imposed upon him by political authority and

public opinion? As for the authenticity, the personal fervor of the voice that runs through the play, we can have no doubts: it is the only explicitly palpable certainty. We shall limit ourselves therefore to this. We are not interested in reconstructing Marlowe's moral physiognomy. We are interested in the play's testimony and in what it generally suggests.

One point worthy of special attention, which nearly scandalizes if it is taken as a coincidence: the passion for knowledge, a theme so central to both *Oedipus Tyrannus* and *Faustus*. The one inquires obstinately about his race, his origin; the other about the meaning and the raison d'être of the universe, which, again, is man's ancestral realm. A quest for paternity in both cases. One could easily make the comparison: passion in Oedipus is existential, in Faustus, metaphysical. This would be a mistaken comparison: in the latter, passion is as existential as in the former, and as metaphysical in the former as in the latter. Both are equally metaphysical.

If Marlowe has added something to the medieval German scrapbook that suggested his drama to him, it is the deeper, total involvement of the hero in the enigma of the world. Faustus and his passion are intermingled; they have become one and the same thing; they are mutually determined. In absolute accord with our initial observation about tragic heroes, Faustus and the action are *one*: his damned quest. Without it, is is impossible to perceive him. He exists for it and through it. If the tragic hero becomes the consummation of his flame, it is because it is the only one that fulfills him in life. This is what is wrong with the anti-tragic in the heroes who survive in the end: they are not organically inseparable from a total passion, hypothesis, idea, or illusion that expresses them. Thus we also understand the inner necessity that dictates the death of the tragic hero. A willed death, because of the author's narcissism or melodramaticism, betrays the hero's organic anti-tragic action.

We see thus, at once, reverberating in *Doctor Faustus*, a play otherwise primitive, the major and defining questions of tragedy. It is exactly this automatic reinstatement of these questions that makes Marlowe's play a tragedy and not its form, which, as we said, is lacking.

Can tragedy exist then in a model that is morphologically incomplete? A tragedy that is not a tragedy? For if it is true that only in the theater — that is, as dramatic form and not as a narrative or any other form — can tragedy be perceived, then form and content must be interrelated. The tragic is not enough as an aesthetic category, it needs a tragic *play* as well.

That this assertion is not arbitrary is shown by the one-sidedness of Marlowe's hero: Faustus and his passion exist inseparably, the identification here is absolute. In life, a person is never defined by one single act, by one single tendency, no matter how imperative. The human person has as his fate mutability rather than inflexibility. The economy of the tragic genre is different. In it, behind the person or the dramatic situation, behind the central emotional knot, lies a "theme" in the sense of an anxiety that contains some meaning, but which is rationally realized. The portrayal of a character does not create tragedy; just as a dynamic confrontation with the adversities of daily life does not create them. A drama can be set up around a central human figure, or around an axis of related situations representing everyday conflict. For tragedy to exist, a special submergence into the space beyond imagistic plasticity is required. The person then, the central figure, the myth, the action, take on the profundity of symbols interpreting the inexpressible. Actions do not constitute the content of the play; "action" does. This action, because of an error in perception and because it testifies to some meaning, has been called *moira*.

Doctor Faustus is at the verge of being and of not being a tragedy. It is saved by the firmness of its subject matter, framed by the two extreme and brilliant parts of the play, its beginning and its end. It is also saved by the intuitive lucidity in the delineation of the central figure, or rather of the diction which it expresses in its innermost world. The insipid rude actions which the enchanted hero commits under an authority borrowed from Mephistophilis are not alien to his nature: This medieval plebian pedant has turned to necromancy, to black magic, because he is consumed by the primitive passion of metaphysical anguish. He is a boor because he is a neophyte. Imagine something similar in Luther, with the addition of missionary obstinacy.

We can now ask whether it is entirely accidental that the ancient poet and the modern one build their tragedies around the question of knowledge. It is accidental in the sense that *Oedipus Tyrannus* does not sum up Sophocles, any more than *Doctor Faustus* sums up Marlowe: it only refers to the question of knowledge in its highest conception. To this latter, which is not so accidental, we can pay more attention.

I would dare say here that the points of view of both the ancient and the modern poet are complementary to each other. This does not mean that each poet lacks autonomy or totality. It means only that the two together present to us a diptych charged with its own meaning.

The quest for who I am and the quest for why I am aim at the same target, although it is unrevealed. Sophocles obscures it piously with the shade of his raised hand. Awkward, rough is medieval Marlowe: he uncovers it momentarily only to cover it up quickly again, frightened by the impiety he had committed. The target in both cases, unconfessed or confessed, is theodicy. Who is the moral culprit in the eternal drama?

To Oedipus' cry "Apollo . . . Apollo, my friends!" Faustus' anguish replies with the echo:

> *Why wert thou not a creature wanting soul?*
> *Or why is this immortal that thou hast?*
>
> (V, iii)

The content in both of these climaxes is certainly different, but in this difference lies its importance. Where the self-restrained Sophocles uses the symbol, that is, allusion (and an allusion is, as we saw, the entire many-faceted meaning of Apollo), frenzied Marlowe allows the direct word to spring forth. Apollo, although called by name, hides the real culprit. Marlowe's Creator, although not expressly accused, is directly called upon to answer for the act of the creation of conscious life, which is consumed by the worldly and by the flames of after-death.

Faustus is the tragedy of God's silence.

In the Christian poet there is blasphemy, however timorous; but not in the ancient. Why?

Thus we arrive at the antithesis *hamartia*-hubris.

The issue is not whether the ecclesiastical authority, in the fearful world in which Marlowe lives, considers the doubting of primary principles as the ultimate impiety. The issue is whether the poet himself contains the certainty of sin in his blood. A certainty that is both terror and magnet, repentance and stimulant. Marlowe belongs to a world permeated with the feeling of guilt, the anguish for an inexpiable crime. Responsible for original sin, he perpetuates it with human imperfection, although the Savior of the world has symbolically redeemed it. He rolls on over the Church floor beating his breast, crying "mea culpa." Waves of generations, centuries of such contrition cannot leave man's sperm uninjured. Marlowe bears the hereditary stigma of an unfree man, born of slaves, who, in order to efface his shame, must deny his own father.

In such conditions the quest, the open and live questioning, is pure madness, deathly sin. Faustus' demand to become a partaker in the Creator's great secrets is expressed in a language which shows that he himself considers his boldness unheard of. Even Mephistophilis gives him answers as if he were the unexpected advocate of Good. This envoy of Lucifer has full knowledge that he represents the Unjust Word; he makes no effort to conceal it:

> For, when we hear one rack the name of God,
> Abjure the Scriptures and his Savior Christ,
> We fly, in hope to get his glorious soul;
>
> (I, iii)

The devils — according to him again — are:

> Unhappy spirits that fell with Lucifer
> Conspir'd against our God . . .
>
> (I, iii)

And to Faustus' question of how it happens that his interlocuter is outside Hell at this moment, Mephistophilis will reply:

> Think'st thou that I, that saw the face of God,
> And tasted the eternal joys of Heaven,

> *Am not tormented with ten thousand hells*
> *In being depriv'd of everlasting bliss?*
>
> 　　　　　　　　　　　　　　(I, iii)

Indeed, a strange temptation, a wretched advocate for the case he has undertaken! Compared to him Goethe's Mephistophilis is a teacher of great cunning, a worthy representative of Evil. Yet, Marlowe's Satan, in his medieval naïveté, expresses a most profound drama: It is the damned soul that commits evil in bitterness, bound to the wheel of its fate, unredeemed, because such is the cross it bears. There is something human, bloodstained, and inconsolable in this dark angel, who journeys along with Faustus, flying low like a bat. Outside Heaven happiness is inconceivable — this is what Marlowe tells us with Mephistophilis' tongue. Darkness is negation, the Evil spirit cannot counterbalance the Good.

A tormented soul, a trembling hand has written *Doctor Faustus*. It pretends to moralize in order to conceal its inner rebellion, to gain passage to the other world. In all this time, it has the feeling that it is sinning, that it is irreparably sinking into blasphemy. The play is a prolonged rending between salvation and ruin, face to face with an eternity that does not forgive. Yet, the tragedy does not rely on this, in its journey; the tragedy relies on the ultimate victory of despair. Marlowe's Faustus is not saved. He keeps the terms of the contract, he pays. No juggling at the final moment, as in Goethe. In Marlowe the price is paid in full, honestly. The struggle with the dark angel has been a fair game.

Compared to the Christian world's tragic poet with the gloomy and torn soul, Sophocles raises an unclouded forehead. His hero's passion is also a quest, a search not ini-

tially transcendental. More human, more direct, Oedipus
is simpler than Faustus; in spite of his royal stature, he
does nothing but submit to a divine decree: to rid his
country of the *miasma*. But entering the game, he forgets
himself. Not even he himself knows the point at which
his search will acquire metaphysical depth. It is rather the
involuntary engagement in a conflict with supernatural
powers that makes him cross over to another level; not the
ambition of his mind. Oedipus seems to have gotten rid
of ambition since the time he confounded the Sphinx. His
purely human drama projects supernatural shadows only
on the imaginary screen in the background.

And his search is unclouded, free from any suspicion of
sin. In the world that created him, his inquisitive spirit
knows not postponements or restrictions. We are free to
ask questions in all directions — to seek evidence even
from the divine. We must know only one thing: that the
game is not without danger. It is your prerogative to accept the risks if you are brave. "Man's measure" is not an
interdiction, it is an apothegm of experience. If you overestimate your capacities, if you are too audacious, you will
be enlightened for your petulance, in a way commensurate
to the greatness of him who surpasses you. The revelation
will be a thunderbolt.

The same outcome in both instances, one might say.
No. Because it is not the fall — a common human fate —
which determines the outcome; it is the play's content.
Oedipus is enlightened to the point of blindness because
of something he had failed to perceive; Faustus pays for
something he knew very well in advance. The path for
the former was open, for the latter, closed. In the first
case we had revelation, "epiphany," in the second, im-
position of a penalty.

*

What part then does this new feeling of sin play in tragedy? Does it enrich or abolish it? Does it add a new note, does it create a new tragic given? If it does, then new harmonies must be heard with this touch of the chord.

It is beyond doubt that the concept of sin opens new perspectives into the tragic universe, provided it is not approached with didactic intention. The sin that ends with the salvation of the soul is a constructive, not a tragic issue. For the causal connection thus revealed between action and outcome subjugates the action to the outcome; it reduces action to a simple presupposition, a "trial." Sin, then, lacks autonomy, it is not man's eponymous action; it is an obstacle placed by God, according to his secret economy. In tragedy, on the contrary, the action and its bearer constitute an inseparable coherence. As we have seen, the one is not understood without the other. An Othello without his "fatal" deception would be absolutely irrelevant to us. Perhaps a picturesque Othello belongs to history, or to anecdote, but the deception with a name, the one that bears Othello's physiognomy, that creates Othello's psychosynthesis, that is what makes him worthy of being a tragic hero. Let us presume the deception of sin not even in its minor Aristotelian meaning but in its major Christian meaning; not inseparable from the person, that is, but devised by an economy from above as a trial. One of the sins, that is, which a man might commit. Right here we have a vivid illustration of ethics; we do not have an ultimate, irreparable confrontation, on an ontological scale, with what surpasses man's limits.

It is here that we touch the edge of the difference between the religiousness of a play and a religious play. *Oedipus Tyrannus*, as we have seen, has religiousness. Implicitly, without categorical dogmatism, without even a rationally clear manner, it suggests speculations that evoke awe. *Doctor Faustus,* though written at the center of the Christian world, allows its hero to bear by himself, as a metaphysically responsible person, the burden of guilt. It does not show him as a factor in an experiment aiming at salvation, at perfecting God's work. Hence its deepest notes of despair, the rending that gives the play its genuine tragic voice. Salvation may exist somewhere, and Paradise, too, but Faustus is not their accessory; he confronts his problems alone, chooses alone, endowed with the judgment and the tendencies that make up his personal existence. Even his Hades appears personal. The Good Angel, the Bad Angel, the Old Man, the other supernatural advocates who appear at intervals to discover him, do nothing but give emphasis and vividness to the terms of the conflict.

Though uneven in form, *Doctor Faustus* cannot also be called immature in conception. It would be more nearly correct to say that it concerns a play that is mature intellectually, but immature in structure. And again, in the word "mature," let us not include the nuances of age. The testimony of an early world, when the Renaissance has hardly emerged from the Middle Ages, *Doctor Faustus* speaks for a conscience that discerns with childlike clarity the main outline of its involvement. Neophyte rationalism and inherited fatalism confront each other passionately. The conflict is dire, though confined to the inner level. The new spirit emerging dazzled into the light, and staggering, becomes conscious of its ultimate dilemma at a glance and denounces it unrestrainedly, without circumlocutions. The two monologues at the beginning and the end are gigantic summations; the one poses the problem, and the other contains the catharsis (which is not salvation). Between these two boundaries parade the allegories, which pay the author's tribute to official morality, nothing more.

Fortunately, allegory in *Doctor Faustus,* with its smothering and invincible language, does not exclude symbol. The meeting with Helen of Sparta is a flash of genius that does not conform with the mythological fashion of an era. Here the new spirit that has begun to breathe over the European world takes some of its deepest breaths. A little earlier, Faustus had uttered one of the most definitive lines of his question: "I do repent; and yet I do despair." It is like a distant echo of the Gospel: "I believe, help thou my unbelief." But it is enough for Helen's ghost to appear, in a splendor of supernatural beauty — a beauty that, let it be noted, transforms the surrounding world, gives it another meaning — for the captive of Hades to swoon in ecstasy. Absolute beauty inspires him with mad hope: "Sweet Helen, make me immortal with a kiss." Two immortalities confront each other here: one by apocalypse, lawful, given; the other independent, problematic, personal. Faustus has become an outcast of the first. What compels him, even for a frenzied moment, to believe that the other can grant him immortality?

Then follows the elation of the soul:

> *O, thou art fairer than the evening air*
> *Clad in the beauty of a thousand stars;*
>
> (V, i)

Beauty here does not have a material quality. It is a value whose essence is purely transcendental, although it has a sensory source. Unconsciously, Marlowe has transcended the level of bold conflicts, of the allegory that simplifies, and subconsciously reached a conception that

surpasses the abstractions: spiritual — material. It is a
third state, beyond the range of the perceptible. We are
face to face with the most hidden achievement of the
New Man.

The meeting with Helen — let us notice this — is a
dramatic advance in the play's development; it is not a
lyrical digression. The final crisis and climax begin at this
point.

This whole moment in the drama is a masterpiece of
inner gradation, a dramatic crescendo. *Doctor Faustus* is
not merely a genuine tragedy. It is a tragedy of the loftiest
order.

A tragedy that poses vertically, definitively, the question
of the absolute. Which poses it in stark but heartrending
language, because it is not abstract like the concepts it
employs. The meeting with Helen, the seeming recurrence
of the spirit of sin heard in the blasphemous inversion,
"make me immortal with a kiss," reveals the awareness
that alongside the profound, perhaps intuitive claim for
eternity, one finds a reality equally profound and firm:
human nature. The former will never come to fruition,
because the latter will always invalidate it. Whoever
thirsts for eternity, whoever becomes worthy of envision-
ing eternity, is exactly the same as he who betrays it. Sin,
thus, is not manifested nor individualized as a palpable
oversight: interwoven with human nature, sin becomes
the determining factor. Faustus appears as the chosen
representative of humanity.

> *Yet art thou still but Faustus, and a man.*
>
> (I, i)

This occurs in the opening monologue, after the achieve-
ments of scientific thought have been enumerated. Hu-

man weakness, in the form of sin, follows us closely like a shadow, everywhere. And here is the outcome: "Ay, we must die an everlasting death" (I, i). There is no salvation precisely because one is a man. The eternal is not realized, because one is a man. Thus speaks the spirit of ultimate despair.

One wonders whether Marlowe's era became conscious of this, whether it understood the real import of such blasphemy. Of course, not even later, especially during the years of Webster and Ford, will the Elizabethans or the Jacobeans lack the courage to accept an inevitable damnation. In the case of Marlowe, however, since the spirit of rebellion has not yet been firmly established, due to medieval theocracy, it is not unlikely that Faustus' external peculiarity passed unnoticed: the audience must have thought that it was a strange, harmless story about a damned magician, who is only relating what he teaches. That is why the hero's final damnation might have been readily accepted: he was a scapegoat. His spectators charged him with their sin, abandoned him to his doom. They did not know that where he was going, he was dragging them along with him.

Above all, they did not know that Hell was shackled to their feet, because it is internal, made especially for man. Yet Marlowe had told them clearly:

FAUSTUS: *How comes it then that thou art out of hell?*
MEPHISTOPHILIS: *Why this is hell, nor am I out of it;*

(I, iii)

Sin, temptation, torment, the prerequisites of eternal damnation, follow man closely; he cannot free himself since he cannot deny himself. The impasse is absolute. Marlowe has not imprisoned his hero in a character, but in human nature. Beneath the magician's gaudy rags exist the characteristics of a person. Supernatural powers, representatives of Hades and Heaven, visions, allegories, all these come as consequences of the metaphysical; they do not define it. Their function bears no resemblance to the picturesque.

And now we see the marvelous line acquiring its full meaning: "Ay, we must die an everlasting death." Everlasting death, this is our lot. Without the assertion that makes me sin, I, a man, would not be a man. I sin, I become blasphemous, I demand pernicious knowledge, with this very same soul thirsting for eternity. Where can I go? Where can I find refuge? To whom can I turn? "To God? He loves thee not." Such utterances had not been heard before. What does it matter whether *Doctor Faustus* is a finished theatrical play or not! It is a testimony that the tragic shudder, after twenty centuries, has permeated the world again. It reappears unified, as in ancient times, with the feeling of the sacred.

Is it necessary for us, in order to recognize in tragedy the authority of continuity, to understand its permanence in Time? If it is, then we should ask what our relation to sin is today. Does it lie heavily upon our conscience as in Marlowe's times? Certainly not. Often today we speak of a "guilt complex," but in spite of all the arguments that abstract it, it concerns something special, psychopathological, and individualized, irrelevant to the historical substratum of our world. We live in a climate of unscrupulousness, unburdened by a sinful conscience.

But if the feeling of sin is anachronistic, the feeling of damnation is not. Damnation without sin, that is what we shall find if we examine the contemporary soul. This sets the tone for the philosophy of our times as well. Not that contemporary man's self-complacency has let him consider himself as perfect or irresponsible. But today the question of responsibility is totally separated from the metaphysical order. We feel accountable to ourselves, to "mankind," to some abstract future, but not to some supernatural commander, who provided us before Time was with sealed commandments.

From this conviction of irrational damnation springs a rebellion of metaphysical dimensions. Consciously or not, we are in conflict with nature. We are ready to ask it to account to us, or simpler still, we consider ourselves its illegitimate child, its apostate, perhaps, in one way or another, an inexplicable or flattering violation, which has no ethical correlation. If one indisputable alienation stands out among the many in fashion, it is this one: our self-exile, our incurable separation from the maternal breast.

But the experience of Marlowe's Faustus is nothing different. Let us not be deceived by the linguistic idiom of his historical moment. Beneath the superstition of sin lurks in him the demand of theodicy. "Why, then, belike we must sin, and so consequently die" (I, i). If death — damnation — is the moral metaphysical consequence of sin, then sin, in its turn, is an ontological consequence of being human. Sin is merely an intermediary step. We are damned because we are men. We die an everlasting death because we are human. Faustus will call to his support Lucifer's battalions because he recognizes that his desperate position is next to that outcast of Heaven, he who once rebelled and was struck by a thunderbolt. From this moment on, Hell is no longer a matter of choice.

Let us repeat: Marlowe's era could not have understood the magnitude of the blasphemy latent in Faustus' tragedy.

It is impossible for its spirit to have comprehended it. If it had understood this, then one might explain the mystery of the poet's assassination. They say that political reasons played a part in it. It was the period of the religious wars, hard to distinguish from the dogmatic ones. But, come to think of it, is it perhaps any different today? The digression from an abstract, ideological, conformist creed was termed sacrilege, an ultimate betrayal. Now the unfettered metaphysics of former times has become coy, has turned prudish: it wanders with its face hidden behind the mask of its adversary: positivism.

VI

The Tragic Error

To Brutus . . . To him he dedicated his most beautiful tragedy.
— Nietzsche, *The Joyful Wisdom*

DAMNATION WITHOUT GUILT is, as we have said, the answer of our time to the complex of sin — the human fate Marlowe has designated. It is worth noting here that the first of these two concepts diminishes man's stature, that is, his cosmological significance, whereas the second magnifies it, even romantically. To be damned, by definition, without personal involvement of your own, shows you to be an unworthy quantity, alien in an alienated universe. Fate is no longer your sin, it is your very fiber. Man's nature, identical with the fiber of the natural world, creates a bondage in the true meaning of the term. We are bound not like convicts but like beasts of burden to the blind inherent laws of materialism, to the wheel of a fate which does not even constitute a deity, as it did in ancient times. We are not graced with the supernatural battling against us. We are crushed by blind accident, an unpropitious hour, which the pyrotechnics of the universe have created, just as they have created us.

But before taking on the shape of guiltless damnation, the tragic spirit passed historically through another formulation or at least another question. Because it relates to the implicit question of the ancient world, as we saw it expressed in *Oedipus Tyrannus*, we must compare these two concepts. I may isolate the latter in its purest form if I examine Shakespeare's *Julius Caesar*.

In *Oedipus Tyrannus* we saw a blatant imbalance between hubris and nemesis. Its outcome relied on the enlightenment the hero receives in the end, that is, in his transference through suffering into another order of values, where measures and standards vary. Tragedy from this viewpoint becomes a revealing experience. Something comparable, although on a different level, happens with *Doctor Faustus*. If we now pass to Shakespeare's *Julius Caesar* we will see that he is gloomier, although he does not have Marlowe's dark colors.

Externally, but also aesthetically, we have here a play full of radiance. The political events, the historical magnitude, the legendary brilliance of the characters, the grandeur of the whole are all well balanced thanks to a most harmonious, wise, and sensitive palette. Rarely has a nobler play been written. How strange: although in the act of the assassination — so brutal, with seven men stabbing one — we witness an appalling deed, the climate that envelops it has nothing of the cruel about it. It imposes upon everything, even upon that very act, its own dominating noble tone. This is not accidental.

Should we perhaps search into Brutus' character for the source of this juxtaposition? Or in Cassius' perhaps, who despite his sickly idiosyncrasy is not, as many consider him, a base soul? To be sure, it could easily have been considered a play of cruelty, with two or three noble figures for contrast. Here it seems that something else is happen-

ing. The nobility of the whole underlines the poet's intention: his dramatic question in the face of the unexpectedly
cruel answer is inspired by lofty motivations. Inexplicable
remains the mystery of the world in which one day we
found ourselves living.

But the answer does not appear so easily. *Richard III*
was the ruin of a man who had inhuman intentions. *Julius
Caesar* is the ruin of two men with noble intentions. In
both plays we have tragedies of the most authentic kind:
their tone leaves no trace of doubt. Which is the common
point that makes these two plays similar? The exceptional
nature of the central characters? But Brutus and Cassius
cannot, in absolute terms, be considered exceptional characters. Thank God, something tells us that variations on
Brutus are not rare in this world, in any period, and, even
less so, variations on Cassius. Shakespeare did nothing to
endow these two heroes with extraordinary characteristics
— and we know very well that if he had wished to, he
could have. He wanted to give them keenness, and he succeeded in endowing them with what is irreplaceable and
indisputable in the lives that bear their names! Nothing
more. It is as if the natural stature of Brutus and Cassius,
the two leaders of the conspiracy, is contained in the inner
economy, in the innermost meaning of the drama.

Two men of good intentions, with a sense of responsibility in public affairs, develop a daring initiative within the
framework of public life; they sin, each in his own way, in
order to serve their ideals; and in the end discover evil instead of good: they end their lives with the feeling that they
have committed murder like common criminals. The ideal
has vanished; only the crime remains. Some dreadful error
has intervened. And this crime now appears twofold in
relation to what the collaborators had contemplated and
accepted: it is not only homicide; it is also futile depriva-

tion of life, for the sake of a fallacious expediency. To such a degree that it becomes Fate — that is, the enigmatic intervention of a third, incomprehensible power. Both men die with the conviction that they are offering their lives in tribute to Caesar:

> CASSIUS: *Caesar, thou art reveng'd,*
> *Even with the sword that kill'd thee.*
>
> (V, iii, 45–46)

> BRUTUS: *Caesar, now be still;*
> *I kill'd not thee with half so good a will.*
>
> (V, v, 50–51)

The revelation here is of a tragic error. But why error? And why tragic?

The answer would be easy if we could see that the man who became the target of the conspiracy was a morally admirable figure, out of the ordinary. Such may seem the Caesar of legend; but he is not quite the Caesar of the tragedy. He appears different right from the start. Nor do we have the right to consider the standards of history or legend obligatory for tragedy. The meaning of the dramatic work is independent from the meaning of history — if we suppose that history has meaning. Tragedy is intertwined around a meaning, albeit an ineffable one; history is created by the course of events. The only thing it tells us is that we live in time and make up a community of interrelated destinies. From the moment the tragic poet isolates an episode in history to turn it into tragedy, it means that something has spurred him, something confined in this isolated chapter, which is completed with it and in it. No reference to the current of history will assure him of an alibi. Tragedy, like every work of art, has aesthetic and moral autonomy.

On the contrary, the opposite prevails. When occasionally Julius Caesar is portrayed by Shakespeare with an ironic or even critical disposition, the implication is that character modification confronts something other than blind history. Perhaps it confronts the value system and sanctity of life; but then the play *Julius Caesar* becomes a didactic parable about any murder; "for all they that take the sword shall perish with the sword" (Matthew 26:52). Is this perhaps the poet's central idea?

Did he arouse the whole of ancient Rome, resurrect an era, open graves, unleash omens, signs, and monsters, to tell us a story that could be illustrated by any middle-class incident whatsoever? Is all this just a picturesque appendage for effect? Or did he perhaps need the dimensions of the legend to give magnitude to the banality of his idea?

At the risk of causing an uproar, we will say that, above all, Shakespeare's precise intentions are objectively irrelevant. What is important is what the work itself says. It is neither the first nor the last time we shall happen to see a work of art armed with the autonomy of a living organism; containing a meaning and dimensions, suggesting associations that its creator did not foresee. Nor in the final analysis can anything prevent the meaning that the work itself suggests to us from being what the poet intended . . .

It is worth noting that in the first two acts, through the intellectual nobility and ethos of Brutus in general, and through Cassius' passion, the play wins us over to the side of the conspirators. The contrapuntal structure of the famous second scene of the first act serves this purpose. It assigns the first dramatic level to the pair Brutus-Cassius, not only from the aspect of intrinsic initiative but also from the aspect of moral interest. Julius Caesar with his retinue is but a din that comes and goes, full of clamor, pomposity, and political hypocrisy of the lowest order:

> BRUTUS : *Was the crown offered him thrice?*
> CASCA : *Ay, marry, was't, and he put it by thrice,*
> *every time gentler than other; and at every*
> *putting-by mine honest neighbors shouted.*
> CASSIUS : *Who offered him the crown?*
> CASCA : *Why, Antony.*
>
> (I, ii, 227–232)

This offering of the crown has all the characteristics of demagogic staging. The trusted friend merely offers the crown so that the honored man can refuse it ostentatiously, and the crowds will be moved.

The offering and refusal of the crown is also mentioned in Plutarch. The offering is done by Antony, but there it occurs twice. The third is Shakespeare's. This is a worthwhile addition if it bears on the general mood of the scene. In Plutarch's *Julius Caesar* the occasion has been organized to test common opinion: A few hired men cheer when the crown is offered; the entire crowd when the crown is refused. Then Caesar realizes that the people are not with him; he rises and gives orders to them to go and dedicate the crown to Zeus, at the Capitol. In Shakespeare, the same scene, with a few added touches, assumes a satirical edge. Now the ridiculous dominates in the gestures of its protagonists.

But this is not the only place where ironic or skeptical nuances appear. The editor Wright remarks that Caesar's hardness of hearing is Shakespeare's invention:

> *I rather tell thee what is to be fear'd*
> *Than what I fear, for always I am Caesar.*

> *Come on my right hand, for this ear is deaf,*
> *And tell me truly what thou think'st of him.*
>
> (I, ii, 211–214)

If this whole ending of the speech with Antony is not
written in a satirical mood, then what should we call
satire? Right after the "for always I am Caesar," and
"Come on my right hand, for this ear is deaf." And immediately, contiguously, the invitation to flattery. Whoever knows about theatrical devices recognizes here one of
the classic springboards of mirth without of course infer-
ring that Caesar is a mirthful person. He is simply full of
weaknesses. A ghostly remnant of his earlier legend, a
wandering shadow of himself, he is a venerable monument
kept standing by the law of inertia. He needs only a push
to crumble. And in fact no serious obstacle arises before
the traitors. Their initiative appears as a historical necessity; the road toward the future, if not toward democracy,
needs to be cleared. At this point in the play, Brutus and
Cassius are almost the instruments of fate.

Will these two men then be punished because the ethics
of history have used them? Or — a new suspicion — do
the inherent laws of tragedy perhaps come into conflict
with the inherent laws of history? If this is true, then it is
in this direction that we must search for the meaning of
the play.

Let it be remarked at once that it will not be a scandal —
not at all in fact — if an antithesis exists between history's
code of laws and those of tragedy. Each aims at a different
end. The one, basically to inform us and, some say, to
instruct us. In what? This is not known. The optimists
strive to derive laws from the flow and interrelation of
historical phenomena. The other, tragedy, God knows

what it aims at. Aristotle has dumfounded us for twenty-three centuries now with his enigmatic "through pity and fear," though lately there are whispers that we should not take this pronouncement as gospel. No one of us can affirm for himself that he has not been sometimes the object of such a purification. We go eagerly to tragedy, we are pleased or bored, we appreciate the performance of this or that actor, of the staging, the poet's dramaturgical skill, the human characters he has conceived, his lofty diction, and at times we even experience some emotion, possibly even awe. In the end we leave satisfied because we have seen something worthwhile, a play, at least, that filled our evening and elevated our souls; but from this to the point where we can talk of a catharsis of passions in the sense of a psychic bath, the distance is enormous. Is it possible that the mystery lurking in us which we call "psyche" finds in tragedy a response that is deeper, more indeterminate or even more ineffable than Aristotle's catharsis? The pronouncements of the great thinkers are needed to open ways, not to close them. There, in the fourth century B.C., Aristotle, with a broad gesture, showed us a direction; he did not close the door. Instead of tormenting ourselves trying to discover what he meant by "pity and fear," it would be preferable to look and see what tragedy itself wants to say. Or, more precisely, not what it means but what it actually says. Because, certainly, it says what we unconsciously ask it to say.

This much only in reference to tragedy's code of laws. For the time being, what we need is to be aware of the asymmetry between tragedy and history. Not an antithesis, then, but a different logic. The tragic poet can use dimensions from history, and set them up as guidelines for his myth. So Shakespeare, too, following the inevitable necessity for history to advance, invests his traitors with its command, and presents, by way of contrast, a Caesar at the moment of decline, thus unleashing the dialectics of his play. Brutus and Cassius do not start out guilty, as Macbeth does before Duncan's murder. They do not have guilty consciences. They start out innocent. And they will end up guilty, or *as if* guilty. This is the "scandal" of the play.

Upon this "as if" is based the whole metaphysics of the tragedy of *Julius Caesar*. The "as if" is Brutus' and Cassius' drama.

They do not have the characteristics of common assassins. Their reversal of fortune, with the final impression it makes upon us, convinces us that it is a tragedy characteristic of the Shakespearian mode, purely and simply because those who pay with their lives are the best. There is no exception to this rule, provided we truly understand the meaning of "the best": not the best morally, which is equivalent to kinder, more virtuous, but human models of a nobler kind, whether good or bad, whether, as we said, of an attainable level or not. At the risk of being commonplace, let us recall that the ethics of tragedy are not the ethics of life. When Richard III falls, or Macbeth, we feel that something rare has been destroyed in the human whole, and that those who stay alive can hardly, all of them together, even with the addition of the element of goodness they represent, counterbalance the loss of the damned man. Things become much simpler when we refer to Romeo, Juliet, or Hamlet. Even great sinners of purple sin, like Othello, Cleopatra, and Antony, leave us with the sense of irreparable loss. This sacrifice of the extraordinary or the noble is one of the secret principles of Shakespearian tragedy, and, furthermore, one of the mysteries of that area of the world accessible only to tragedy.

But are we contradicting ourselves? We had said, a while

ago, that Brutus and Cassius are not extraordinary natures, and that this "natural" stature of theirs appears to have been foreseen by the inner economy of the play. It is as if the poet wanted to show that the *impersonal good* is condemned when it comes into conflict with some unrevealed order of things, and that it is not so much the star of Brutus or of Cassius that demands that they pay blood tribute as it is the circumstance expressed by their lives. Judged from this standpoint, they do not resemble the tragic heroes we saw in the first chapter; they are not exclusively and solely defined by their fatal action. They also exist independently of it, as distinguished citizens of Rome.

It is indisputable that Brutus and Cassius cannot be compared with Hamlet, Othello, Lear, or Macbeth; but they can be perfectly compared with Romeo or Richard II — without the crown. Thus we see the appearance of another order of tragic heroes, determined not by an innate absolute so much as by the fatal stands they take in life. General circumstances have trapped them, carried them away in a vortex. Their tragic virtue ensues from the way in which they confront the challenge and react to the crucial act. They elevate the critical event to the dimensions of tragedy because they give it meaning through the total offering of the supreme good: their lives. It appears as if they had proven themselves worthy at the crucial moment of unexpectedly rising to the stature of tragic hero.

If we look around us, we will see that the same happens in ordinary life: persons of ordinary dimensions suddenly in special and unforeseen circumstances emerge as heroes. If circumstances did not demand this, they would end their lives quietly and insignificantly. The exceptional event is what is needed to bring to fruition their latent potentiality. Brutus and Cassius, Romeo and Richard II, bring tragedy to our dimensions. They show that tragic grandeur is not a category outside the analogies of life.

But does not the ancient theater also have such heroes? What else are Iphigenia and Polyxena? If the other numerous plays of known and unknown tragic poets of the ancient world had come down to us, we would be able to include other similar characters in this intermediate category, in which sacrifice at a crucial, unforeseen hour is the only feature shared in common with the absolute tragic heroes, along with the uplifting of the soul.

Finally it is worth noting that these sacrificed beings counterbalance their lack of physical grandeur with an innocence or at least with something unconscious that characterizes them, and which gives their loss a particular pathos.

Does not something similar also happen with the two heroes in *Julius Caesar?* No one doubts the innocence, naïveté almost, of Brutus. But even Cassius, the seemingly invidious, neurotic Cassius, what else is he but a fiery soul, created to be consumed by its idée fixe?

It is amazing how at every moment of this play the bell of fate is heard tolling, nearby or in the distance. When we talk about fate in tragedy, we should bear *Julius Caesar* in mind and not ancient drama where other notions and forces — *Dike* (Justice), *Ate* (Folly, Rage), *Ananke* (Necessity) — are brought to mind by the poet.

In reading *Julius Caesar* (and we say "reading" because it is not at all certain that the performance, with the frequently superficial innovations of mise-en-scène, will easily justify these suspicions), one has the impression that invisible and unverifiable forces operate behind the events, the characters, the situations, the historical scenes. No other Shakespearian play seems to unwind on two levels at once: the perceptible and the mental. Although a political drama, *Julius Caesar* — the first perfect example of the genre, and valuable in this sense as well — is incessantly illuminated by supernatural visions, premonitions, prophecies, an atmosphere of destruction, that make the characters feel they are partaking in something incalculable. The political drama here is broadened to the cosmological.

When correctly examined, the conflict between Brutus and Cassius in the fourth act, at the critical point where it is placed by the poet, and with its inner interrelationships, acquires a profound eloquence. It is the beginning of damnation, the implicit, virtually symbolic foreshadowing of condemnation. Anyway, its protagonists sense it darkly, intuitively; their minds turn constantly to Caesar. A split is revealed between them, but it will not materialize as in the case of Macbeth's progressive separation from his lady after the first murder. Murder here does not have the same vicious, unredeemable intent (and that is why "Hell" here is not "murky!" [*Macbeth* V, i, 39]). Yet, behind the violent disagreement that breaks out in Brutus' tent, one senses that superior dark forces are functioning, transforming the characters into puppets.

In the last act, right after Cassius' death, the poet seems to reveal, if not the meaning, at least the leading thought of his play. It is strange that he has entrusted this passage to Messala, one of the third-rate characters of the drama. But in another sense it is natural that a third person guess and express the meaning of a reversal of fortune that had as its main symptom the darkening of the minds of those who had become its protagonists. Messala says to Titinius:

> *O hateful error, melancholy's child!*
> *Why dost thou show to the apt thoughts of men*

The things that are not! O error, soon conceiv'd
Thou never com'st unto a happy birth,
But kill'st the mother that engender'd thee!

(V, iii, 67–71)

For the heedless spectator, Messala's abhorrence seems inspired by Cassius' death, the outcome of a misconception concerning Titinius' fate. But neither Messala nor Titinius knows at this point the reason for Cassius' suicide. Pindarus, the only witness, has disappeared. And it is true that Messala's first line refers to the general disbelief, to the shattered morale of his friends over the outcome of their deed:

Mistrust of good success hath done this deed.

(V, iii, 66)

But such disbelief has not been manifested from the start of the conspiracy. It began appearing, with us seeing the events from the outside and with a clear eye, from the moment fate pronounced the verdict. Thus, Messala's abhorrence reaches beyond the specific event to meet with the main story. According to Messala, the cause of Cassius' deception is melancholy. Melancholy: one of the four "humours" which, according to the beliefs of the times, determined human personality. Yet Cassius' psychic state would justify other sorts of characterization: He is irritable, neurotic, sullen, fanatic, grouchy, passionate, whatever you wish, but not melancholic, or "a moody soul." With such idiosyncracy one cannot set up a conspiracy that aims not at personal revenge but at the abolition of despotism, at a reversal of the current of history. Our mind then rises above the immediate events, to encounter another pattern, another instant or mood, at the beginning of the play.

Act I, scene ii: Caesar and his retinue have made their first exit from the stage. Only Brutus and Cassius have remained:

CASSIUS: *Will you go see the order of the course?*
BRUTUS: *Not I.*
CASSIUS: *I pray you, do.*
BRUTUS: *I am not gamesome: I do lack some part*
Of that quick spirit that is in Antony.
Let me not hinder, Cassius, your desires;
I'll leave you.
CASSIUS: *Brutus, I do observe you now of late:*
I have not from your eyes that gentleness
And show of love as I was wont to have;
You bear too stubborn and too strange a hand
Over your friend that loves you.
BRUTUS: *Cassius,*
Be not deceiv'd: if I have veil'd my look,
I turn the trouble of my countenance
Merely upon myself. Vexed I am
Of late with passions of some difference,
Conceptions only proper to myself,
Which give some soil, perhaps, to my behaviours;
But let not therefore my good friends be griev'd —
Among which number, Cassius, be you one —
Nor construe any further my neglect
Than that poor Brutus, with himself at war,
Forgets the shows of love to other men.

(I, ii, 25–47)

Brutus begins with the "melancholy" we will also meet in another Shakespearian hero not so kindred to him, although some say so: Hamlet. Brutus is internally prepared to welcome an announcement and instigation like those

Cassius is soon to propose to him; otherwise, the very self-controlled and thoughtful Brutus would not so easily have agreed to join, much less to lead, a conspiracy of such historical responsibility. If Cassius had not found Brutus in such a mood, he would not have spoken to him, at this moment at least. But we remember Cassius' exhortation and unjustifiably forget the mute provocation Brutus represents.

> CASSIUS: *Then, Brutus, I have much mistook your passion;*
> *By means whereof this breast of mine hath buried*
> *Thoughts of great value, worthy cogitations.*
>
> (I, ii, 48–50)

These important matters would never have been unearthed if Brutus' attitude had not encouraged them. Cassius starts speaking vaguely, inviting his friend to look into his own countenance. He makes a brief speech of praise, in tune with the public's understanding. And immediately comes Brutus' answer:

> *Into what dangers would you lead me, Cassius,*
> *That you would have me seek into myself*
> *For that which is not in me?*
>
> (I, ii, 63–65)

In vain he insists that he never had such thoughts; he had something more decisive, the predisposition to listen. He reveals no fear whatsoever, no turmoil, when Cassius exposes his idea explicitly. His first reaction is this:

> *That you do love me, I am nothing jealous;*
> *What you would work me to, I have some aim:*

> *How I have thought of this, and of these times,*
> *I shall recount hereafter.*
>
> (I, ii, 161–164)

He has been thinking! He is burdened with something that has been stirring within him for a long time. And it will not long be necessary to postpone his announcement. When the conversation is over, after the interruptions of Caesar's appearances and the interference of the scene with Casca, Brutus himself will eagerly say to Cassius:

> *Tomorrow, if you please to speak with me,*
> *I will come home to you; or, if you will,*
> *Come home to me, and I will wait for you.*
>
> (I, ii, 309–311)

At the end of the next scene, Cassius speaking to Casca will state that "three parts of him/Is ours already" (I, iii, 154–155). Brutus is on their side. And the next day directly, about daybreak, finding Brutus sleepless in his garden, we will hear him opening his soliloquy like this:

> *It must be by his death . . .*
>
> (II, i, 10)

Cassius had not spoken to him about murder . . .

All this does not intend to throw the burden of responsibility exclusively upon Brutus' shoulders. Its purpose is to explain the role his psychic disposition and predisposition will play psychologically and *theatrically*. In a performance we see this at every instant, but not in reading the play.

Is this consciousness of responsibility? Is it sorrow for

the need to sacrifice a significant being, who personally is not indifferent to him, but, on the contrary, is friendly? Is it prepaid remorse? One way or another, the fatal "error" Messala will mention at the end has for its starting point this predisposition, a pessimistic psychic landscape full of gloomy premonitions. It is as if there exists in the world a fatal error belonging to the man born with a human psychosynthesis, which becomes the sole cause of catastrophe for its bearer. If we do not have here an absolute identification of the tragic hero with the action that will realize him and plunge him into the depths, we have his identification with an error equally determining of his singularity. But are not "error" and "action," in essence, one and the same thing? Othello's action is his "error." Macbeth's action — Duncan's death — is his error because he believes that he was born to reign. The act of murder at the Capitol is Brutus' error in believing that he is freeing Rome. And finally, what is this error but what Aristotle had once called *hamartia,* which bears no relation at all to the same Christian concept founded on a dogma, but meaning a reckless thought, a weakness, a faulty evaluation of what is right?

The entire tragedy of Oedipus is the story of a fatal error.

And now arises the great, the crucifying question: who instigates this fatal error?

Is it perhaps the offspring of blind, unintelligent fate? Does the combination of circumstances in the plays under discussion leave us with this impression? How can the strange stature of the heroes be explained? As victims of fate, should they not suffer something lamentable, humiliating? Would not each one be a "plaything" in the hands of chance, a figure unworthy of admiration, not inspiring awe in you, not to be called a hero, but whose spectacle would be repugnant, for he would have killed whatever dignity life has, even the most chimerical? A mousetrap! That would be an appropriate characterization for the universe we live in. It is the epigram that the theory of the Absurd has chosen as its motto. That is why the world of the Theater that bears its name, in spite of its metaphysical glimmerings, is by definition anti-tragic. Nor does it deny this.

But we will not have enumerated the crucial givens of *Julius Caesar* if in the roster of its values we do not record another theatrical value, unique of its kind: Marcus Antonius.

He is exclusively worldly. All the other persons of the play, primary or secondary, are more or less accompanied by an aura, a kind of astral body following them in their course, which shows them shuddering at times. Brutus, Cassius, Julius Caesar, Portia, Calpurnia: each has a personal, inseparable shadow, projected and beckoning on a mental screen. On the contrary, Mark Antony is bathed in a profuse, Mediterranean light. Sculpturesque, firm, realistically effective, the master of his actions, he does not fail for a moment in any of his calculations. Playing a dangerous game, he proceeds without questioning, and this convinces us that in the innermost economy of the play, he bears the responsibility for counterbalancing all the others with his material weight. The victory will be his, because the world is his physiologically.

Brutus is an ideologue, Antony a politician.

Mark Antony, a vivid figure, captivating in his vigor, a necessary factor in the structure of the tragedy, remains organically anti-tragic. He will become a tragic figure in his own play, when, paired with Cleopatra, he will also enter a fatal dance of errors and weaknesses. Here, he is only strong. His mission is not to err, but to be justified by the events and prevail over them. Only incidentally present in the first half of the play, he towers after the first half, at the moment of catastrophe, and dominates from that point on. He is the sword *Dike* throws onto the scale to provide the solution. Julius Caesar, no matter how ghostly, would have remained unrevenged without Antony. Antony revenges Caesar, but in order to win the victory for himself. Surely, the usurpation is not his doing. It is life's economy that is at fault.

It is as if the conspirators have worked and damned themselves for the sake of Mark Antony . . .

Seen in this light, the play presents an unexpected ethics which is *pronounced* by tragedy: the sinners pay the tribute of blood, a fact which, tragically, expiates them; but a third person, who has become the viable instrument in the hands of *Dike*, benefits from their drama. Life's reality is not won by the man who pays honestly; but by the one life favors. We live in a tragic world to the extent that its standards are not our standards. Tragedy here is the fatal juxtaposition of the human standard with life's inhuman one.

This is not a definition, it is not the final conclusion. It is a useful observation, which sheds light at this stage of our course. Mark Antony over Caesar's body, when the conspirators have left, evokes an ancient Greek concept — the only absolute concept mentioned in the play:

> *And Caesar's spirit, ranging for revenge,*
> *With Ate by his side come hot from hell . . .*
> (III, i, 270–271)

Ate's name is appropiate to Mark Antony's speech, des-
ignating a force coming from afar, out of the preclassical
world, and charged with tradition and wrath. What is
Ate in the archaic conception? The personified blindness
of mind, the cause of every tragic error, *hamartia* proclaimed as a deity. It is a projection and reflection of
transcendental temptation within the human conscience,
which reflects it as confused, and unable to provide a
logical explanation.

Thus we encounter, indirectly but also categorically, the
controversial problem of evil.

They say that tragedy is the representation of evil, and
they mean in its broader, metaphysical manifestation.
This view seems satisfactory at first glance. Some evil, or
some evil person, as a rule provokes the tragic spasm:
Richard III, Macbeth, Iago, Goneril, or Regan. This does
not involve abstract entities, it involves living beings, instruments of evil. And let's forget that Satan is the personification of evil, or still worse, its incarnation. Of
course all the cases we have enumerated come from
Shakespeare, but this is not the point. Marlowe has con-
tributed, too — even more expressly in fact — to this abstract concept with his Mephistophilis, who is very naïve,
as we have seen. And in ancient tragedy we have Clytemnestra, Medea, Odysseus in *Philoctetes*, the ancestral sins
of the Atreids, of the Labdakids. But let us limit ourselves
for the time being to Shakespeare: In *Hamlet* there is
Claudius; in *Macbeth*, the Witches, if not he himself and
his lady; in *Othello*, Iago; in *King Lear*, Goneril, Regan,
Edmund. In all these works at the poet's climactic hour,
evil appears incarnate. In *Julius Caesar*, a play so close
to Shakespeare's great period, where is the evil?

Incarnate, concrete, it appears nowhere. Does it perhaps

not exist at all? This does not seem probable either. On the contrary, we have the feeling that evil flutters around silently, indeterminate, and because of this all the more enigmatic and disquieting. It is something like an impersonal and inconceivable plot, which is manifested through the characters without any one of them becoming its exclusive bearer, but forcing the two arch-traitors to do whatever is necessary in order to become its victims. It is a perfidious evil, which deceives in order to lead astray, smiles momentarily in order to lull to sleep, envelops itself in the glowing vestment of an ideal, and suddenly, at the crucial moment, reveals its horrid countenance. How can Brutus and Cassius confront it since they are impregnated with it unconsciously, mingled as it is with their loftiest aims?

What then can the morality of such a tragedy be? No matter what, the play that poses a moral problem suggests, willingly or not, a certain moral confrontation, merely in the way it presents the events. As we have seen, the presentation of events in *Julius Caesar* provokes many questions. Does this mean that the poet wished his play to leave such a fluid impression?

Nothing excludes the possibility that Shakespeare *wished* it less fluid than the way we view it today. Many earlier examples reveal this in his conscience, the conscience of a man living in an era just emerging breathless from the dreadful Wars of the Roses, when every possibility of anarchy inspired terror. Better a ghostly authority preserving the lawful order than a relapse into the nightmare of civil war. On the first level then, it is not unfitting to attribute such a thought to Shakespeare in reference to *Julius Caesar.*

But we have said that a perfect work of art, sailing

through centuries, lives a life of its own, independent of the poet's circumstantial intentions. *Julius Caesar* survives in the degree that it transcends these intentions. It is as if the play had two faces: one turned toward its poet stating to him that authority as authority expresses a high necessity, reinforced by the sanctity that imbues the lawful order (Sophocles would have supported this view, probably, if we could ask him), and another face turned toward us, faintly illuminated by the enigmatic smile of the Sphinx. If the play were imprisoned in its own period, it would have only one face. Since it shows us a second face, we have the right to ask ourselves what this smile the monster shows us is telling us.

It tells us that within the tragic world intention is not measured by the principles of human ethics. It tells us that this world we live in is tragic because it cannot be tamed by our system of values nor is it appeased by our moral claim. It also tells us that if things were different, we would not be talking about tragedy. It tells us that in this ontological conflict of values that constitute man's inner law, in contrast to the undecipherable law of the world, what is noblest has no consequence, but vanishes more surely than the basest. It tells us, finally, that justice lies in the peculiar radiance the heroic emanates at the moment of the catastrophe. Only this has been granted to man: the chance for a final flame, consumed by its very own existence. It is a tragic action because it does not have a practical counterbalance. It is a tragic action because something unique, irreplaceable, is being sacrificed. A negative universe, with its positive pole some Other World, a place of refuge, of reward and justice, would not allow any possibility for tragedy. But tragedy is not an object of choice. It is imposed by the order of the world —

upon those worthy of living it. What is chosen is the ethos: to rise to the tragic with one's courage, or to succumb fatally.

Perhaps it is time to realize that the fatal qua fatal is not tragic. Perhaps it is time to free tragedy's realm of the despairingly monotonous and meaningless preconception of Fate, which is intended to provide answers to everything without explaining anything. "Fate" is an easy alibi, a shunning of the battle.

Many, we are told, have seen Fate stooping down over *Julius Caesar.* Most probably, what casts its shadows over this Shakespearian play has an even more enigmatic face, because it is much less mythical.

VII

The Tragic Ecstasy

Cypris . . . primal mother of the human race.
— *Seven Against Thebes*

My hands are pure, but my mind has some pollution.
— *Hippolytus*

THE TRAGEDY of the passion for self-knowledge, the tragedy of God's silence, the tragedy of the indecipherable *Dike:* all these, and still more, which we have gathered in the course of our study so far, are not at all separate utterances; they are the complementary colors of one unified tragedy, which seems to have been playing since time immemorial with an unpredicted outcome. This in any case essentially differentiates "drama" from tragedy: we have as many dramas as there are circumstances. But there is only one tragedy, though with different masks. Drama has social, tragedy ontological substance.

Modern times have introduced a theme that clearly appears to be their own. Although the ancient world did not ignore it, modern times have introduced it in the sense of giving it scope and an almost representative emphasis. We must consider purely incidental the fact that only Euripides' *Hippolytus* has come down to us from the ancient world as a tragedy of love. Neither *Medea* nor *The Trachiniae* can be considered pure tragedies of love. In the former, revenge dominates, in the latter, something like it. We do not call it a tragedy of love, but a tragedy in which love changes into something different, into a by-product. But *Hippolytus* is from beginning to end a tragedy of love, the tragedy of Phaedra's passion, with Hippolytus as its object; Hippolytus who is no longer Phaedra's victim, but Aphrodite's. Here the tragic lies. Hippolytus is punished by a higher will whose law has been disdained. Hippolytus, as Phaedra's personal victim, would be the subject for a drama, not for a tragedy. A social scandal.

Thus *Hippolytus* remains unique in ancient dramaturgy. Lost are Sophocles' *Phaedra* and Euripides' *Sthenobia* and *Phoenix*, and who knows how many more plays by tragic poets who themselves have not even survived. What distinguishes the modern world, then, is not so much the new illumination of the subject as the persistent dedication to it. After the Middle Ages, starting with the troubadours, the theme of love, when it is not dominant in literature — dramatic, narrative, or lyric — blends with others, often to subjugate them, but mainly to warm them with a lyricism that the modern soul demands persistently, on every occasion. In our postwar era, which affects an assertive, irreconcilable cynicism, the erotic element is not only not absent, but even assumes pathological dimensions, becomes almost a psychosis. "Our entire civilization," Bergson has said, "is aphrodisiac."

In this sense, the erotic theme would have historic and

not tragic meaning if it did not happen to engender in itself something transcending literary treatment. We are used to seeing in the love story a suitable given for plot and action: Two persons meet, fall in love — without ever knowing why, because there is no "why." Expectation begins, the mutual quest, but something intervenes between them, the lovers meet obstacles, until the obstacles are removed by triumphant love, or the persons succumb. There is also a unilateral variation, where only one person is in love, and the other resists, because he has other aims or other ties, and from this disparity ensues a depression ending in suicide, separation, or revenge. In either type of amorous involvement, if one is a little careful one will notice that love is not the main theme, although it appears so. The main theme is myth. Love has become an element in the synthesizing of a myth, a motivation for representation and action. Representation in action.

But if there is something deeper defining love, it is its innate thirst. The reproductive instinct appears, as we know, armed by Nature with an especially radiant and attractive array, while its face is persistently covered with a mask. As a natural need, erotic desire is disproportionate to all the other natural needs. Hunger and thirst, the daily functions of the body, are all imperative and inviolable, but they are not accompanied by this excitement and elation, this transubstantiating capacity or dark passion. They do not lead to poetry. They do not intoxicate the person who experiences them nor touch lyrically a third person who sees them being enacted. Love uses a charm of its own and leads into warm participation. Some would certainly say that this reveals that we are dealing with the most fundamental of all instincts, the one that perpetuates life. Our task here is not to examine it mechanistically; it demands our attention a priori. And we will immediately distinguish love tragedies from the tragedy of love. It is a distinction corresponding to what we said before: love as dramatic motivation vs. love as dramatic thirst. Love as personal symptom vs. love as impersonal testimony.

Let us say from the start that in the theater, all the models we have at our disposal belong to the first type. We can put them in order, using qualitative distinctions as our guideline: Euripides' *Hippolytus*, Shakespeare's *Romeo and Juliet* and *Antony and Cleopatra*, Racine's *Phèdre*, and perhaps Don Juan as a figure, or rather a symbol, beyond the characters of Tirso de Molina, Molière, Zorrilla, and their successors. From all these, we shall limit ourselves to those plays that have a tragic taste. Not because the others are not worth mentioning, but because they have nothing in particular to teach us. The love element has a fundamentally tragic character. It is the subject of this chapter.

In Euripides' *Hippolytus* love is encountered as a natural force; natural and invisible. If the charm, the radiance that the central figures, Phaedra and Hippolytus, emanate were not so intense, we could say that this tragedy arouses the problem of freedom and responsibility: it is very clear from the start that Aphrodite sets the trap and manipulates the strings, as she explicitly states in the prologue of the play.

But the goddess withdraws to make room for the drama, and from the moment the drama begins we forget her. We need the characters to remind us of her with their instinctive digressions. Thus, the proper impression is created that through the characters we relate to higher forces, and not through the higher forces to the characters.

For the contemporary spectator what happens to the Aphrodite of *Hippolytus* happens to the Apollo of *Oedipus*

Tyrannus. Whether we see or read the play today, we find ourselves at an absolute disadvantage in transcending the mythological presumption, the staged phantasmagoria that wants the goddess idolatrously tangible. This is unfortunate. Aphrodite — a beautiful woman, immortal and ageless, with a sufficently scandalous past — is a character appropriate for an operetta by Offenbach: she inscribes the play from the start in the wrong musical key: the supernatural character of the goddess is limited to her fairy-tale power to charm invincibly, to transpose herself without obeying the law of gravity, like a fairy in Andersen, to dwell on Olympus, and easily satisfy all her desires. All these are the projections of human wishes, as always in a fairy tale; they do not partake of the irrational. With such presuppositions, and the parallel ones relating to Artemis — an untamed tomboy who roams unbridled over mountains and gorges — *Hippolytus* appears surrounded from beginning to end by an agreement that has at best the grace of a picturesque masquerade. With this, the pedestal of tragedy has been demolished.

How can we today recall the awesome, immediate feeling of an incontestable power imbuing the universe? At the most, we could accept nuclear energy or electricity. How can we touch the pulse of universal desire, from the throbbing of the leaf to the very sap that rises and nurtures whatever is living? To the secret shudder of youth? Our life has been forever imprisoned in artificial fabrications; we have stuck a label, inscribed an algebraic formula, on everything. Ancient man, even when he was uneducated, could revert to the supernatural, which was for him the soul of the natural:

> *Cypris roams in the air, exists in the stormy sea,*
> *and all things are born from her;*

> *she is the one who sows and gives us Eros*
> *whose children are all of us on earth.*
>
> (447–450)

It is the Nurse, who is Phaedra's nanny, speaking, not some mystical poet. Or rather, poetry here is created spontaneously and simply out of amazement and awe before the miracle of the world. The educated, the Nurse tells us, bow even lower before the works of the "demons," because they have heard, learned more:

> *Those who possess the writings of the ancients*
> *and are with the Muses always,*
> *know how Zeus fell in love*
> *with Semele; they know how radiant*
> *and lovely Dawn snatched Cephalus once*
> *because of her love; yet in heaven*
> *they dwell and do not leave the gods . . .*
>
> (451–457)

And the Chorus:

> *Eros charms the one on whose frenzied*
> *heart he descends, winged, golden gleaming.*
> *He charms the wild beasts of the mountains,*
> *the creatures of the sea, those the earth nourishes*
> *and the bright burning sun watches,*
> *and men; in royal majesty, you*
> *Cypris are the only ruler of them all.*
>
> (1274–1280)

Everything bows to this cosmogonic force, gods and heroes: "Pleased, I think, to submit to their destiny" (458).

*

No analogy at all with the go-between who was Juliet's Nurse. In the Nurse we have the pious conformity of an experienced soul, who knows that resistance to the will of the goddess is a sin, to be paid for in a dreadful way:

> ... and this is nothing else but hubris,
> the wish to be greater than the gods ...
>
> (474–475)

Impiety means offense against Nature. Cypris is an invincible enrapturing goddess, but also relentless, who does not conform to moral human demands:

> ... Cypris, then, is no god,
> but something greater than god ...
>
> (359–360)

This testimony of the Nurse, that Aphrodite means something more than a goddess — if that can be — is awe-inspiring. We are in the realm beyond good and evil, where implacable truth draws breath. Truth here is not what is in accordance with human criteria, not the "moral."

This testimony of a world beyond moral order lies at the foundation of ancient tragedy and, if we consider it closely, of the tragic soul in general. From the moment we wish to garnish the phenomenon of the world, subject it to human categories, tame it in order to make it comprehensible or consoling, we have entered the sphere of ethics, but we have lost irrevocably the taste of tragedy. We accuse the ancient pantheon for its anthropomorphism, but we forget we have also given human expression to the universe, since we wanted it organized according to an inherent law that expresses us. This, and not the ancient anthropomorphism, is the reason why we can no longer discern behind and beyond the Aphrodite or Artemis of *Hippolytus* what these figures symbolize. We see ideas, not forces. The allegories hide their meaning from us. Our mistake lies in *thinking* that what is signified will become more familiar, because we will make it comprehensible whereas it has ceased long ago to be familiar to us.

The second obstacle in a contemporary approach to tragedy is the translation of the ancient text, in whatever language it is made — Modern Greek or foreign. The structure of the language is not the vestment of thought. Language is the thought itself. Things begin to exist from the moment we name them, even within ourselves, in an unutterable way. Each language has its own inner economy, which is interwoven with the psyche of an entire world — its own world. The ancient word, transmitted into contemporary language, seems more naïve than what it actually was; or rather, its naïveté changes character. Its sober and pious, compact and stark eloquence turns into something close to nonsense or gossip; in foreign languages it is burdened with affectation, a quality so alien to its fiber. We forget that two and a half thousand years cannot be bridged by good intentions. Nor by wisdom. What the ancient world held most precious, ethereal, genuinely poetic, remains eternally shut off from us. Only intellectually can we approach it. And again . . . as a French critic remarked recently, when we translate ancient poetry, what does the greatest damage is not piety, but its opposite: familiarity. In trying to convince ourselves that what was said then is eternal, we bastardize it with contemporary verbiage that is hardly natural or

spontaneous. Translation, instead of bringing ancient tragedy closer to us, moves it farther away. It turns it into
something belonging nowhere, neither to the past nor the
present.

After this measuring of distances, what can we say is
salvaged from a play like *Hippolytus*? An idea rather than
a poem. Let us at least see what the idea says. This tragedy
of Euripides, one of his most beautiful, could be entitled
"Eros Dynast." Phaedra, a fiery impatient Cretan maiden,
originating in a mythical realm, haunted by the Mino-
taur's breath, is seized by a violent erotic passion for her
stepchild. He is young and she is young, closer in age to
him than to her husband. Often in the play she is addressed as "o child," not of course as a little girl but as a
maiden. And she is called this not only by the Nurse, who
when she wants to address her as "my child," calls her
"my little child," but also by the Chorus, the young girls
of Troizen. But Phaedra knows perfectly well the obligations demanded by her position as stepmother and queen.
A noble nature, full of dignity — Albin Lesky says, "a
great lady" — she chooses to pine away with longing
rather than violate the sacred bonds of her marriage to
Theseus. Her passion, as we shall see, is more erotic yearning than the erotic storm that bursts forth, burns, and
singes. An introspective, tormented love, Phaedra's desire
makes the heart swoon. She reaches the point of envision-
ing the Gates of Hades, in a trembling dim light, as the
only way out.

This feeling has been created by Euripides with marvelous passion and sensibility. Humane in its warm and
distressed substance, there is something that elevates it at
the same time: Hippolytus is not an ordinary mortal. The

son of an Amazon — of Antiope? of Hippolyta? — he also
hides in his blood something emanating from elsewhere,
from a race beyond the dominion of men. It is not accidental that we see him as an initiate into the austere worship of a goddess who is an everlasting virgin. The un-
tamable and the unearthly reside in the blood of the
Amazon's son. We perceive him inflamed by a thirst for
galloping in forests, with his hair in the wind, and drunken
eyes. A sullen contemporary author, poisoned by systematic psychology and bookish wisdom, would have made
Hippolytus sexless or complex-ridden, the victim of some
Freudian neurosis. But Euripides moves in the free realm
of myth. With his Hippolytus, the winged inspiration of
the open air steps on stage. This fresh breeze will accompany the young man through the course of his life, and
will not leave his lips except with his last breath.

Thus ancient tragedy is always quantitatively balanced
with equal ingredients from the world of men and the
universe of the demigods. Tragedy is not a bird that flies
low. To men, it brings what gives an answer to their deepest desire: to transcend the human. Where later drama, in
making "life," constantly rebuffs, imprisons, prohibits,
tragedy frees and gives wings. Those who have said that
its level is disdainfully remote from the human have no
idea what man's secret psyche conceals within itself.

But Phaedra's love for Hippolytus is not opposed by
some natural discord between them, in the way that Racine will alter it later. The French poet, in his eagerness
to write "psychology," abolishes the tragic, brings it down
to the waxed floor of court drama. His Hippolyte is in
love with someone else: Aricie. In Euripides Phaedra's
love is of the pure eros-*hamartia* kind; Phaedra is bound
to Theseus, piously dedicated to her obligations. Hippoly-

tus is her husband's son: the foretaste of adultery thus takes on something of the tinge of imaginary incest. This is the crime. It is encumbered by the vow of chastity of Artemis' worshiper. It is as if a queen had fallen in love with an anchorite; deities are involved in the drama, and something profane is about to occur.

However, all these complexities — and let us be careful here — emanate from the characters. They bear no relation to original sin, religious morality, or prohibitions dictated from above. The heroes are by definition free; what they believe and what they live in they themselves have chosen. Phaedra, in her despair, blames her blood, the lot of her race destined to offer victims to Cypris:

> *O unlucky mother, what a strange love was yours!*
>
> (337)
>
> *And you, unhappy sister, Dionysus' wife.*
>
> (339)
>
> *And I the ill-fated third one, see how I perish.*
>
> (341)

She can refer only that far back; this is the only in-depth projection of her passion. She gives it something not unholy but mythical. The crisis, therefore, will be restricted to the plane of human dignity. This is what makes Phaedra actually sin at the last moment, at her death, and resort to slander, to salvage her wounded pride and dignity:

> *But she, afraid lest she be dishonored,*
> *wrote the false writings, and destroyed*
> *your son through treachery . . .*
>
> (1310–1312)

Artemis says this to Theseus at the moment of "epiphany" — the moment of truth. It is worth noticing that, although the heroine herself and the other characters of the play refer back to Cypris as the cause of the evil, yet each assumes his responsibilities personally. The will of the goddess is an explanation, not an excuse. There is no moral alibi.

What does this mean? It means that the content of the symbol of the ancient divinities is very clear. Cypris or Dionysus, writes Jacqueline de Romilly, these impeccable masters, have something akin to human instincts, against which it is dangerous to start an open war. Not human instincts; natural forces rather. They do not constitute personal or even supernatural wills, functioning independently from the wills of the tragic heroes. Aphrodite exists, lives in Phaedra's blood, just as she lives (the Nurse and the Chorus have told us) in the waves of the sea and the seeds of all the beings of the earth. Is it fate? Is it *hamartia?* Fate presupposes condemnation, *hamartia* an initial, "original" error, the "fall." But Aphrodite's law is interwoven with the nature of the universe, does not constitute a punishment, nor thereby lead to some kind of salvation. Ancient man accepts the world order as something unified and given, indicative of a superior, inscrutable economy. He accepts the miracle of the world and his own place in this miracle, and a mortal's ultimate duty, *sophrosyne:* to know and revere the laws "high on the pedestal," as the Chorus in *Oedipus Tyrannus* has called them.

Hamartia then — in the Aristotelian sense — personal, not of the race to which one belongs, nor of mankind. The difference is that whereas in the dogma of original sin man is under the repression of a given guilt, which he must redeem with his lifelong service in this world, viewed as a place of trial, in the ancient religious framework the error is not determined; each of us can avoid it. *Moira* is unleashed and operates when someone through personal error provokes it. Then *Dike* is indeed manifested relentlessly. Then, if the error is very grave, it can follow the guilty blood from generation to generation. Ancient tragic causality is cruel because it has as its prototype life, which is cruelty itself. But it is not arbitrary. "He who chooses is responsible; God is guiltless," Plato has said (*Republic*, 617e). The responsibility lies with the person who chooses, not with the god. You are free to choose.

These differences are not stressed here to show the possible superiority of one world over the other, the ancient over the modern. Each has its historical raison d'être. The differences are stressed to make it perceptible where the soul of tragedy lies. And because after a certain point its path was lost. It was a path that did not lead to the Lost Paradise, as a Nietzschean romanticism might have eagerly maintained; it led instead to a natural world, virginal, but also ruthless, like Nature. A fresh world, but also desperate. Earthly life is for it the only certainty, and the feeling of nonrepeatability is inconsolable.

> But if there exists something dearer than life,
> it is surrounded and concealed by dark clouds.
> We seem to love desperately
> what shines brightly on this earth,
> because we do not know and we have no proof
> that there is another life under the earth;
> and thus we are swept away by such fables.
>
> (191–197)

The Nurse's words say something definitive. The nature of ancient tragedy is based on this consciousness, which,

as we have observed in the first chapter, is but an imminent lamentation.

Euripides restricts the study of the tragic in love leading
to destruction and lamentation to Phaedra. His Hippolytus remains emotionally nonparticipating, unassailable,
because he is also organically alien to Aphrodite's law. He
serves the regime of another goddess. But how can such a
thing happen, since the law of love is universal and inviolable? In this lies the young man's error. Without any
morbidity on his part or even moral infirmity — in fact,
on the contrary, *because* of his unrestrained vigor — one
might say the Amazon's son consciously violates his duty
to Aphrodite. He seems to have disciplined himself so well
in the life of the open air (the association with horses, the
endless hunting, the wastefulness in the embrace of the
natural world) that he feels no need for a sacrifice to Cypris. He not only ignores the passionate goddess, he even
despises her: "No god worshiped in the night pleases
me" (106).

The gods who are worshiped at night are not loved by
Hippolytus; he is the irreconcilable child of the day. His
indifference to the divinity of soft life and nightly orgies
reaches a contemptuous mockery: "To your Cypris I say a
long goodbye!" (113), he says to the old servant, who is
horrified at what she hears.

This is his impiety. Hubris in the form of impiety. It
seems superficial, childish in its frivolity, but it reveals a
deeper rebellion. Cypris will make Hippolytus her target;
his punishment is the drama. Phaedra is sacrificed mid-
way, as a means to the necessity of serving the vengeance
of the goddess:

> But Phaedra, though honorable, must die:
> I do not set her misfortune before

vengeance on my enemies,
that I receive the honor that I deserve.

(47–50)

says Aphrodite in the prologue. From this also stems the passionate character of Phaedra's love. Outwardly, the love-sick queen does not act, except with her death and with her accusation before Theseus, which is confused with the act of suicide. The same resolution dictates both.

Phaedra is blond like Aphrodite, although she comes from the South, from dark-skinned Crete. To Greece she brings something exotic. Euripides is not concerned with human geography; he therefore does not assign to his heroine the color of her land; he wants her to have the color of the myth. Phaedra and Hippolytus are select beings, both carrying something from the remote past sufficient to elevate them to the pedestal of tragedy. She is the daughter of Minos, he the son of an Amazon. The "philter" — which in later centuries will acquire such luster with its supernatural qualities, especially in the medieval love stories — appears here for the first time. The Nurse, seeing the torment and madness of her mistress, will remember the "soothing philters of love" (509–510) that she has hidden in the house. She will remember them in order to cure her. As the French commentator Meridier currently observes, the language of the Nurse, at this point, is of double meaning: it suggests the "charms and words of enchanting spells" (478) that obliterate passion as well as those that satisfy it and inspire a corresponding desire in the beloved person. Anyway, the Nurse's reasoning is eloquent:

For if your life were not so miserable,
and you were a prudent woman,

never would I have led you to this point
merely to satisfy your pleasure and lust;
now the great struggle is to save your life,
and this is beyond blame.

(493–497)

Yet, Phaedra's reaction also says a lot: "I fear lest you be too clever" (518). She fears that the nanny's adroitness will go beyond the limits, that is, violate them, offering her what she longs for with all her senses.

But the philter will not be used. The Nurse's intention inexplicably remains unaccomplished. While the old woman has undertaken the responsibility for further action with an eloquent and categorical "Let that be, o child" (521), she enters the palace to employ worse means: to speak to Hippolytus as a go-between. After this the catastrophe is guaranteed. Only Phaedra's physiologically weakened resistance justifies her allowing such a thing to happen. Her weakened resistance and her subconscious hope of despair.

The abandonment of the philter that would have evoked mutual love assures the verisimilitude of the myth, but also abolishes the mystique of the theme of pleasure. Love is no longer the communion of souls in a twofold leap toward the unattainable. Tragedy as a humanistic monument gains, but a gap is left unfilled — it will remain for centuries, perhaps forever, with one unexpected exception, though in a different, skewed direction, a musical drama of the nineteenth century: Wagner's *Tristan and Isolde*.

Euripides' *Hippolytus* is a love tragedy, it is not the tragedy of love. The difference is this: as we said at the beginning of this discussion, the erotic phenomenon has a fundamentally tragic character; it is one thing to incite tragedies through erotic passion and another for this erotic passion itself to be a tragedy. Ambition, hatred, jealousy, rancor, revenge, and the other recognized passions and sentiments, tested as dramatic motivations, do not have an innate tragic fiber. They may or may not be able to climb the tragic pedestal. The erotic phenomenon, even when it does not know it, even when it frolics with itself, has a tragic character.

What deceives us in the erotic function is not its fulfillment; it is its deceptive appearance and its everyday consumption. Fulfillment has an extrinsic face, a mask that almost covers its other, intrinsic one. One sees people of both sexes satisfied, sexually balanced, and forgets the secret hour of the gasping uphill path, the spasms of the damned, the continually renewed and reiterated anguish that will last as long as there is the vigor of life in the human race. The exercise of this function balances the organism, but it does not reveal the secret of love. It conventionally restores something like a lawful order, necessary for social coexistence. But the subversive forces, the dark and dreadful dynamism, loom in the depths, lie in wait with fiery eyes. We feel this with periodic relief, like volcanoes which intermittently erupt, releasing the pressures of subterranean fire.

Everyday partaking seems to tame the face of the wild mystery, pretends to enlist it in a mechanism of smooth and controlled function. Something repeated every day seems flat, tame, neither dangerous nor incomprehensible. Yet, it is precisely with its incomprehensibility that every analysis of erotic fever should start.

We know this fever and we experience it, but we do not know why it exists, or where it aims. The answer that it aims at the "perpetuation of the race" is a tautology, not an explanation. A most stupid tautology indeed, because it employs the twofold argument of natural law and of poetic splendor. But something that is reproduced merely to be reproduced, is either absurd — and therefore tragic in being desperate, or is deceptive — therefore tragic in being inscrutable. Let us not seriously consider the proposition: "perpetuation as a means for the gradual perfection of the human race." Evidence of such ultimate apotheosis has not been given us, and all living beings are reproduced without such ambition. Nor would there be any meaning in the perfection of a being destined to perish anyway, to be destroyed by Nature itself, which created and processed it through much trial and error. But if such an assumption is really true, then it would be doubly tragic, because it reproduces values without counterbalance, condemned by definition by laws qualitatively incommensurate with them, and blind as well.

The tragic element on the erotic plane is inevitable.

From this brief examination we come to the conclusion that, one way or another, "reproduction as an end in itself" is held suspect by tragedy. The only conceivable escape would be an attitude of moral mockery toward this vicious circle. Contemporary nihilistic theater resorts to such an attitude. The place of tragedy is taken by tragicomedy, King Lear is succeeded by the puppets Clove and Ham. But let us not forget that this is not an evaluation, though it appears so. It is an emotional reaction: indignation in the form of a theory of life. Something like blasphemy finding relief from an unbearable psychic burden — or psychic void. Tragedy was an evaluation — the "absurd" is spite. In tragedy there is no barren metaphysical rebellion; there is contest, strife with the metaphysical.

Prometheus' torment is a dialogue with Heaven; so is King Lear's on the night of the storm. If in Prometheus we saw only the rebel, we would immediately place him on a lower rung, the one Beckett acknowledges for his heroes. A rebel is a slave who wants to overthrow his master because he envies his privileged position. But Prometheus questions the superiority of Zeus as a free being, and Lear rightfully invokes the assistance of the Supreme Judge, whoever he may be:

> O heavens!
> If you do love old men, if your sweet sway
> Allow obedience, if yourselves are old,
> Make it your cause; send down, and take my part!
>
> (II, iv, 192–195)

This is the genuine tragic cry: it does not hesitate to name the Unknown. It does not think it has obliterated the Unknown or punished it by denying it every title. Beckett's Godot is not only an absence, he is also an abstraction; Oedipus' Apollo and Lear's Heaven are substances, personal litigants in the ultimate trial of universal tragedy.

If we now return to the level of physiological function that constantly reproduces this trial, we will see that it has the paradoxical stigmata of contradiction: the erotic action is a knot of two four-legged animals of the lower order; its rhythm is mechanical and blind. But at the same time, before starting the steep uphill path that will lead — both interested parties know this beforehand — to a leap into the void, a revelation takes place somewhere in the depths of being, a transubstantiating vista: something like an inner vision flashes, bathing the viewer with light. The presence, the existence of what is symbolically called "psyche," becomes never so tangible as in the moment of beastliness. It exists because it reaches the brink of nonexistence. Is it accidental perhaps that in an inconceivable moment it invokes death as its unique fulfillment? When the uphill path nears the point of fulfillment — a split second before the spasm shakes the root of life — something appears to half-open and to close again immediately, like a window onto an invisible, enchanting view. The groan that accompanies this trial, the blending of blissfulness and pain, of triumph and moan, seems to bear witness that what is taking place surpasses both the capacity and the fortitude of man. If it lasted a little longer, the heart would break. What collapses exhausted on the mattress afterward, with the feeling that it was fooled, that it failed at the leap, is again a heavy animal, fettered at the wheel of Time. And only the existence of a true and great love for the companion of the opposite sex, the accomplice, can save this moment from unconfessed shame and despair, transform it into something serene: affection, gratitude, tenderness — all compensations for an exodus that failed. As for the feeling of satiety that deceives some, those whose eyes are open know perfectly well that it is a temporary substitute, a petty reward for the target they are unable to reach, are not even allowed to guess. You come back no wiser than when you set out, like Faustus, for Knowledge. But with the sole suspicion that perhaps something unattainable exists. The very same act helps you to forget it, and take it for its opposite: the ephemeral.

This is the secret element of love. It is accompanied by the feeling of dreadful anguish. Of a composite and varied anguish: now the quest for the beloved person; now an undefined mystery enveloping it, both enchanting and disquieting; now a twofold effort to reach the unattainable target; now the disappointment of failure at the leap; now a futile thirst for communication; now the defeat of an entire erotic life; now the impression that what you have sought and adored in the beloved was a deception. The anguish is extinguished only when love is also extinguished. And again, in the erotic act that has remained a mere semblance, an empty mechanism, or in bought love, some residue will remain, a shred, a parody of the voyage, merely to testify to a miracle that is not realized even symbolically. It is the mirage in the desert, the irony in place of Paradise.

All those who in a thousand ways are inflamed by desire, by sin, who sacrifice themselves, who kill, are killed, who deceive, strive toward this experience. Not, as a nearsighted "realistic" spirit would maintain, for the perpetuation of the race. The fanatical pursuit, the invincible motivation, is a momentary transubstantiation, a test run for the leap. Minds of the highest caliber, like Schopenhauer or Nietzsche, have never shown less magnanimity than when they saw in erotic desire a trap for the perpetuation of life.

The erotic mystique is the announcement of possibilities and conditions we cannot reach. Euripides, the skeptic who expresses the twilight of a virgin world, the godless poet, knew something when in the tragedy of Phaedra and Hippolytus he made a confession of faith to the goddess rising from within the liquid cradle of life.

VIII

Beneath the Star of Death

THE LOVE EXPERIENCE is a boundary situation in the sense Jaspers gives to pain, struggle, guilt, chance, and death. If we are inevitably subjected to these five concepts, at least they concern situations with concrete faces and identities. The love experience is a twofold enigma. We discern the first, the nearest: reproduction; it is impossible for us to penetrate the second. At times, something tells us that it exists, though invisible. And at other times, it seems something deceptive, insubstantial.

What can we do to try to set foot on solid ground, without straying into metaphysical revery? Attest to the most tangible things, but without didactic, much less encouraging or moralistic, intention. We perceive this then: perpetuation of life equals perpetuation of death. The two are identical. Perpetuation of death equals perpetuation of pain. If there is a trap, it has been set so that I may transmit the flame of the consciousness of my finitude, and my pain — a determining element of my race. Nature's aim, most probably, is not my aim; or if it is, I do not know it.

In the erotic force we discern a strange longing for eternity. Not a pro forma eternity, but a qualitative and poetic eternity. And this longing for eternity ends in the creation of ephemeral beings. These beings advance gradually, within a historical framework, outside any eternity. For this reason, if I transcend the usual superstitions, I will see that in love, real love, there is always something desperate: a passion for boundlessness, a thirst for the absolute, ultimately insubstantial and unfulfilled. Where there is no thirst for the absolute, there is no genuine erotic passion; there is carnal excitement, mechanical imitation of a function that now appears symbolic. That is why genuine erotic passion is always accompanied by the feeling of anxiety, as we have said — a soft-voiced or loud anxiety that belongs to the extrinsic symbols of passion. Through the body that we adore, it seems we wish to forget our own body, and transcend it; to submerge into what holds it together and is imperishable, beyond the authority of Time and the grave. The ritualistic element in love has magnitude and religious Dionysian spirit. They think they disarm it when they destroy its cause, by ridiculing the erotic act, and defaming woman, who thus becomes a cheap and easy prey. The delusion is comparable to its opposite: overstimulation spurred by deprivation. A mystery ridiculed is not a mystery solved. A parody of the known has taken the place of the unknown. There exists a tragedy without consciousness, without grandeur.

Although it does not appear so, love is a defeat. Those in love aim at one thing, love aims at another. To be precise, lovers do not know what they are aiming at. They thirst for pleasure and exaltation; it ensures perpetuation. They aim at the immaterial. The lovers envision the perpetuation of happiness; love realizes the perpetuation of happiness through deception. Thus love terminates in the perpetuation of pain and happiness; like beauty, they appear ironic; not that at a certain moment they were not realized, but because they were measured — by definition they demanded to be measured — with the measure of the absolute.

The absolute is innate in genuine love. And love, objectively, can be perceived only in time, outside the dimension of the absolute. This contradiction establishes the tragic in love.

Contemporary consciousness has perceived another aspect of the love tragedy: the attempt for a deeper penetration into the world of fellow man, a world akin to me, sharing the same fate, yet which remains impenetrable. The mania for an essential intermingling, a need for existential communication, beyond the conventionality of speech. Contemporary mores have mechanized the erotic act with the hope of thus breaking the idol and penetrating the barrier of delusion and myth, and reaching a direct rapport. Above and beyond idealization, they have sought the starkness of truth. They were faced with a truth that not only was not sought after, but that resembled another delusion. Exiled, we accept the fact, the defeat: we obstinately dress ourselves in the rags of a shipwrecked man. This means resignation in the place of decisive action. We started out programmatically stripped of sentiment, and through another path we reach a bare sentiment. The defeat is twofold.

Let us return then, for a methodical reconnaissance of the territory, to the nearest source. There, at the conscious starting point of our world, is found the dramatic poem of total love, in the tragedy of *Romeo and Juliet*. In it the reveries of the troubadours and the desire that intoxicated the Renaissance are historically distilled and crystallized.

We say "source," we say "conscious starting point," but

E. K. Chambers — one of the few authorities on Shakespearian matters — notes before anything else that when
Shakespeare sat down to write this tragedy, the legend of
the "immortal lovers" had already been formulated. As
examples Chambers enumerates Paris and Helen, Troilus
and Cressida, Hero and Leander, Antony and Cleopatra,
and from the medieval legends Tristan and Isolde, Lancelot
and Guinevere, Paolo and Francesca, Abelard and Heloise.

But it is obvious that Chambers has in mind a different
category from ours. The groups of lovers mentioned above
are woven, through the length of centuries, by anonymous
legend, not by identified art. They are typical and im-
provisatory. Homer did not deal specifically with the loves
of Paris and Helen or Troilus and Cressida: with a small
anaemic epic poem Musaeus has helped the common consciousness create the myth of Hero and Leander; and
Antony and Cleopatra take a place in the realm of art,
become monumental, only when Shakespeare comes to
immortalize them with the tragedy that bears their names.
Before Wagner Tristan and Isolde were essentially legend.
Lancelot and Guinevere, Paolo and Francesca come into
existence, acquire civil rights in our poetic heritage, because of Dante Alighieri; but it is well to remember that
in the *Divine Comedy* they have a place organically equal
to many other damned persons, and their treatment there
is descriptive, concise. This means that so many pairs of
lovers, including Abelard and Heloise — who are not artistic creations — are merely the subject matter for the treatment, and the gradual crystallization of the spirit, of the
legend. We cannot ask them for anything more profound.
When they do not function in the symptomatic, non-
aesthetic realm of minor or major history, they are proverbial types.

The tragedy *Romeo and Juliet* is the epigrammatic expression of a spiritual value, even more the creator of a value in which poetry has condensed a meaning of life. This means that in it we can search for human depth, something both broad and unrepeatable, as a synopsis of the beliefs of a whole world, recording in a critical moment its personal testimony. It is noteworthy that this achievement has a designated character: it is created by a great dramatic poet and not by the consciousness of common men. This consciousness, whenever creating myths of love, produces static, schematic combinations. They are like algebraic equations, representing an abstract sentiment.

That is why we speak of a starting point. A starting point that is also a summation, a summary of the erotic passion as the fingers of the troubadours have embellished it on the chords of the lute, as the first worthy poets of the Renaissance — Petrarch and Dante — beheld it. Shakespeare has legends before him, not works of art. That is why his work maintains such freshness.

The tragedy of *Romeo and Juliet* is what Jung calls an "archetypal myth," a fundamental form. If we see the play through the prism of art, we realize immediately that a representative and immemorial experience of man has found here its absolute expression and balance. This is what makes the pair Romeo and Juliet partake of legend. Yet they transcend it, because ultimately they become a work of art of the highest order. Theirs is a reinforced legend, imperishable as much as anything human can be imperishable, a definitive legend.

Neither the course of historical life nor the imagination of generations can alter it. In the progress of collective life the figure of Faustus or of Don Juan changes; each generation of men elaborates upon these symbols, alters them in order to entrust to them its personal experience or dream. Romeo and Juliet are given, established; we accept them as they have been immortalized once and for all; they are prototypes. If we suppose that tomorrow, or some day, man's nature will be fundamentally changed through the intervention of eugenics, the pair of young lovers from Verona will vanish the way a whole continent or a ship with all its passengers sinks. With them they will take, if not the last word of man, at least the last word of a world.

The Chorus that speaks the prologue of the drama offers two key words. These lovers we are going to see, it tells us, are "star-crossed" and their love is "death-marked." These two concepts will degenerate later in the hands of imitators; they will become the "fatal" love, and the showy literature of the "love-death" diptych. We must ignore this continuation, efface it from our consciousness, in order to be able to see this tragic pair of children with fresh eyes.

However, the words "star-crossed" and "death-marked" cannot be translated. It is not because of the inability of a language other than Shakespeare's to render them, but because there are some concepts interrelated and reciprocally dependent on the words that first brought them into the light, that is, incarnated them. God created the word with the power of his logos; language, in poetry, is a creator: it does not formulate, it conceives and testifies.

One way or another, the two young lovers will be marked, from the start, crosswise by a star. Which star? This is shown by the word "death-marked": the star that sets the seal of death upon whatever it illuminates. Capulet's daughter and Montague's son have been born beneath the star of death; and it is here that another, deeper "why" is expressed: Could it be because the two families are in conflict? Could one perhaps imagine Romeo and Juliet married like ordinary people, sinking carefree into the swamp of conjugal life, bearing children, raising them, and growing old? One can imagine such things about characters in drama, about the heroes of Ibsen's *Wild Duck*, for example. Hjalmar, Gina, Gregers are characters on an ordinary level: they exist within the framework of everyday life; we can imagine them in different places and situations. But not Romeo and Juliet. They exist outside everyday routine, beyond the laws of common experience. They were born to fall in love and to die from an inevitable love, which, one could say, in its hidden essence, while revealing the deeper meaning of the human, at the same time is not of this world. Outside this absolute love and outside death, which is the complement of this love, Romeo and Juliet do not exist. They were born to illustrate the yoke *love death*, to suggest its hidden meaning.

It is noteworthy that this fate, although the poet is conscious of it from the outset of the play — as are the characters — never becomes meaningless rhetoric about fate, never boasts. The conflict that opens the action, apart from being a brilliant device intended to arrest the spectator with its plastic eloquence and set loose the rhythm of the turmoil that is the dominant note of the play, also suggests its twofold meaning: an irreconcilable conflict altogether and a game with death. The dark figure of Tybalt, already emerging at the seventieth line, will reverse the deceptively ludicrous conflict of the servants, and he will disclose the real, the abhorrent voice of hate:

> *Turn thee, Benvolio, look upon thy death,*
> (I, i, 73)

says the gloomy swordbearer to the peace-loving but weak Benvolio; and he draws his sword.

This first conflict will be quickly suppressed by the intervention of the Prince of Verona and remain hidden but lurking from then on, preparing ruin. The situation that now has been established for the entire play is the rule of hate. And on this gloomy background, it will begin inscribing gently, in enamel colors, the story of young Romeo's soul. Indirectly at first, through the words of his own family, and later with his appearance on the stage.

The contaminated breath stays in the air. Romeo smells it:

> . . . O me! What fray was here?
> Yet tell me not, for I have heard it all.
> Here's much to do with hate, but more with love.
>
> (I, i, 178–180)

Then follows that rhetorical eloquence with its extreme antitheses which will later be the basis for so many modifications (until its climax, in the Romantic phase of the nineteenth century, with Victor Hugo). Except that they do not bear the mark of an original. There is also the union of forces that will act in the development of the myth, provoke, by their chemical synthesis, the explosion, and the crisis:

> Why then, O brawling love! O loving hate!
> O any thing! of nothing first create.
> O heavy lightness! serious vanity!
> Misshapen chaos of well-seeming forms!
> Feather of lead, bright smoke, cold fire, sick health!
> Still-waking sleep, that is not what it is!
>
> (I, i, 181–186)

This is how Romeo bridges the gap between the conflict that he sees before his eyes, and his momentary erotic
illusion:

> *This love feel I, that feel no love in this.*
> (I, i, 187)

Because Rosaline, who remains unseen to us, is one of
the Capulets, the enemy clan, to which Juliet also belongs,
as we are to learn later. Romeo was born to love: such is
the mission he is entrusted with — by whom we do not
know. They say that his character is not clearly drawn.
But that is precisely why: he is the ideal bearer of love.
They also say that he represents the impersonal portrait
of any eighteen-year-old. But how many eighteen-year-olds
resemble Romeo?

What does he know himself? Something he unconsciously says at the beginning, in the stream of his speech,
which in a more critical moment, even before the end of
this first act, will acquire its real meaning:

> *When the devout religion of mine eye . . .*
> (I, ii, 93)

Religious faith. This is Romeo's reply to Benvolio's con-
tention that the Capulets' feast will shine with beauties
whose radiance will overshadow that of Rosaline.

> ROMEO: *When the devout religion of mine eye*
> *Maintains such falsehood, then turn tears to fires!*
> (I, ii, 93–94)

The continuation here has no meaning per se. It is a
bet made to be lost. But when we hear Romeo's first words

to Juliet, we discover that a strange mysticism exists in the soul of this youth:

> *If I profane with my unworthiest hand*
> *This holy shrine, the gentle sin is this;*
> *My lips, two blushing pilgrims, ready stand*
> *To smooth that rough touch with a tender kiss.*
>
> (I, v, 97–100)

And a little later:

> *O! then, dear saint, let lips do what hands do;*
> *They pray; grant thou, lest faith turn to despair.*
>
> (I, v, 107–108)

We live in an irreligious century that mocks such worshipful outbursts. Yet it would be good to remember that if man no longer idealizes love and does not deify women, he still continues to deify men: politicians, demagogues, swindlers, pseudoprophets, football players, nightclub singers, movie stars. We believe that we have been saved from the worship of heroes because we have transferred our worship to another plane. Now we have hero-worship in the extreme; man has always deified man. But what matters is not the object of worship; it is the worshiper. Religious feeling is that which *I* feel, not what the person who has evoked it feels. Not what the person called upon to invoke it in me feels.

If Romeo is not simply any eighteen-year-old youth, neither is Juliet simply any fourteen-year-old girl. Here the otherwise marvelous H. Granville-Barker is mistaken — even if one takes his words as a figure of speech: "The boy and girl — they are no more," he says about Romeo and

Juliet. Of course, in this he wants to stress their generality, or rather their representative meaning. But generalization is dangerous; it simultaneously discounts the category to which the two young lovers belong. If Romeo is proven capable of such love, a Juliet, not a Rosaline, must be found too. Rosaline is an illusion: she is what we invest in love and in the beloved, without their generating or sanctioning it. In fact, in this we see that in the transference from one girl to another love acquires true, deeper meaning. Juliet, in her seeming naïveté, is that paradoxical being who is worthy of becoming the object of worship touched with religious mysticism. The meeting of the young Montague with the tiny Capulet (this has been noted and recognized by many) resembles the manifestation of the divine called "revelation": Something beyond the union of the representatives of the two sexes. Something beyond the every day, typical function of reproduction, however poetically idealized. We are allowed to wonder what would have happened to Romeo if a girl like Juliet had not been born in Verona.

Again, the passionate Montague might have fallen in love with some other girl; but we must certainly doubt that his love would have the elemental intensity of the absolute, and the unutterable meaning of the diptych love-death. For the tragedy of *Romeo and Juliet* to exist, we need a Romeo and a Juliet; accordingly, if we view the play narrowly, we have merely a drama of characters. The fortuitous coincidence of these two children, amid the general circumstances of the moment, makes something unexpected tangible for us. Something unique, beyond any love story, no matter how beautiful.

If Romeo and Juliet were two lovable children, but of a more common type, we would have a drama, not a tragedy.

Even if the enmity of their families has pushed them to death. We must understand this clearly. It is neither the poetry nor the romantic climate nor the double death — or even the triple death, including Paris — that makes the story of the two lovers of Verona a tragedy. It is the personal fiber of its two heroes and whatever is revealed to us through this personal fiber. The elation is theirs: it has not been added by the poet, as is the case with bookish tragedy makers. The inhospitable climate of hate could have been a symptom. Then, we would have the didactic conclusion: here's where men's blindness, malice, or folly leads. But this is not the case. Here the inhospitable element is as organic as love. It is *intrinsically* necessary to the realization of the secret phenomenon. Love is illuminated through death, death through love. Only in such circumstances can Romeo's meeting with Juliet acquire its real meaning, just as the erotic act between two lovers acquires a special quality in the dark of night. The ecstasy in love of the two children of Verona is inscribed upon the dark background of hate just as it is also inscribed upon the sacred night that shows Juliet " a winged messenger of heaven" in the eyes of her Romeo.

But to create this precious phenomenon, even the specific persons of Romeo and Juliet are not enough. It is also necessary for them to be of the proper age. A little later, and it would have been too late. The poet insists upon the age of his heroine; and as for the age of his hero, keeps reminding us of it, constantly and eloquently, through his language and attitude.

On the first plane, the central theme of the play is love as conciliator. More especially, the juxtaposition of love and hate and the recognition of love's superiority. If we look closely, however, we will see that this moralistic thought obeys something deeper. The play's secret lies in some *moira* within the figures of the two heroes, perhaps without the poet's full awareness — so true it is, indeed, that a genius can overreach his logical intentions.

The first point we must note is that the two central characters find their destination in love: love provides them with unique and complete fulfillment. They are realized through love.

But not through love alone. An emotion like theirs evokes something surpassing the circumstances, the potentialities, the nature of life. Romeo notes this unconsciously, the instant he sees Juliet for the first time, though she is still unknown to him. Shakespeare's line here is unique in epigrammatic expression and vibration. It is definitive:

> *Beauty too rich for use, for earth too dear!*
> (I, v, 51)

Is it accidental perhaps that only six lines later we hear the first thunderclap from Tybalt's mouth?

> *This, by his voice, should be a Montague.*
> *Fetch me my rapier, boy.*
> (I, v, 58–59)

That is how what will later appear to be the organic outcome of this love is signified on the obvious level. Such a psychic state cannot be fulfilled except by death. There are projections of the inner world, projections so absolute, passionate, and ultimate that we feel they transcend the limits of the attainable.

Such extreme feelings we will often encounter in Shakespeare. They are boundary conditions that because of their very nature attract death as complement and culmination. For example, the overflow of Othello's soul, when he finds Desdemona again, after the tempest that separated them:

> *... If it were now to die,*
> *'Twere now to be most happy; for I fear*
> *My soul hath her content so absolute*
> *That not another comfort like to this*
> *Succeeds in unknown fate.*
>
> (II, i, 192–196)

But death in the tragedy of Romeo and Juliet is soon to have a double face. It is the fulfillment of the unfulfilled and it is darkness. Again, Romeo will become conscious of it that very night at the Capulets' ball, when he learns who the girl is who has pierced his heart by her mere presence:

> *Is she a Capulet?*
> *O dear account! My life is my foe's debt!*
>
> (I, v, 121–122)

And fifteen lines later, Juliet, guessing that the quake she has felt within her is to be the definitive one of her life, speaks in a monologue, waiting for the Nurse to tell her the name of her beloved:

> *... — If he be married,*
> *My grave is like to be my wedding bed.*
>
> (I, v, 138–139)

He is not married, but he is something worse. Thus, the prediction of the maiden will acquire a double power.

Death is enigmatic, a two-faced Janus; it appears in this play both as savior and executioner. The nuptial night of the two children will unfold a few hours after Mercutio's and Tybalt's dual murder, that is, under the shadow of death. The two children embrace in the midst of blood-shed, they embrace in despair. It is a union-separation. And the erotic ecstasy in Juliet's virgin bed will also become a pretaste of union in death.

ROMEO: *I must be gone and live, or stay and die.*
(III, v, 11)

Let me be ta'en, let me put to death.
(III, v, 17)

Come, death, and welcome! Juliet wills it so.
(III, v, 24)

JULIET: *O God! I have an ill-divining soul:*
Methinks I see thee, now thou art so low,
As one dead in the bottom of a tomb:
Either my eyesight fails or thou look'st pale.
(III, v, 54–57)

ROMEO: *And trust me, love, in my eye so do you.*
(III, v, 58)

This bears no relation to the nineteenth-century narcis-sistic literature that will blend love with death for maudlin reasons or have an empty melancholy as its object. This is not sentimental self-indulgence or self-adoration. It appears that before man's eyes a secret relation is being revealed for the first time, uniting in a supreme reality two pairs of counteracting forces: perpetuation of the race and

annihilation, and the thirst for immortality and the ir-
revocability of the moment.

That Shakespeare envisioned this love as something absolute, unique, extreme, is also suggested by the special
quality of his poetry: It is not a vestment for the play or
the characters. It is the national language of lyrical passion,
containing a message in its very essence. At moments one
wonders whether such lines can ever be satisfactorily delivered. The verse plays of the French theater, both classic
and Romantic, can be delivered with pomposity or plain
emphasis or singsong; they are part of rhetorical speech.
Italian verse sings by itself, carried by its melodic fluctua-
tion of cadence. In this play Shakespeare's lines have a
hidden radiance, more intense than their surface one. If
they are delivered with extrinsic musicality, they will be
sacrificed; if with deliberate prosaicness, their glow will be
extinguished. It is as if the poet, at the moment of writing,
forgot himself entirely in order to live fully the stage vision
and not the stage action.

Romeo's speech, for instance, which opens the balcony
scene, must burst forth like a delirium in order to justify
and sustain what follows. But in this internal torrent, if
the words, the images, the concepts are not articulated,
then alas! The poet has organized the overflow of his hero's
soul theatrically, with syncopations, changes of rhythm,
transitions; yet all these are unable to sustain the fervor
of his speech. The flashes of lighting that penetrate him
belong to adoration, to spiritualized pleasure, gentleness,
ecstasy, exaltation, intoxication, and above all the childlike
dazzlement before the mystery's epiphany, which makes
him shudder and which until now the young Montague
did not suspect lay in the blood of life. If all these are not
utilized, the speech becomes a drawling tirade of theatrical

rhetoric, incapable of preparing for the duet in the garden at night. A similar observation applies to Juliet's precious monologue in Act III, opening scene ii:

> *Gallop apace, you fiery-footed steeds . . .*

It is the enchantment of a girl in love, but expanded by the galloping of a young heart rushing to break its fetters. If the images from Greek mythology here did not soar winged into the dimensions of myth, fired by the imagination and vision of the young girl, they would chill the scene's emotional surge, and turn it into pedantic similes. They mingle quickly with memories from the Nurse's fairy tales, perhaps as the little girl heard them in her chamber. Such is the personification of Night that Juliet's persistent invocations call up. This is not the rhetorical device of a mature tragic heroine. On the contrary, Juliet has the unconscious credulity of the little girl who has not yet cut herself off from the world of the nursery, and who believes, in her critical moments at least, in powers and spirits that haunt nature.

Generally the diction of this tragedy, if it does not give off the breath of mysticism, is reduced to verbalism and redundancy.

Yet, after this analysis, we are allowed to ask ourselves if death can be considered a metaphysical complement of love, so that the tragedy of Romeo and Juliet can also be the tragedy of love. If we take the external conflicts as the main element in the play's central idea, then the play is not the tragedy of love. The conflict between the two families is a social factor. It is accidental. But if we consider what is fundamentally unattainable, metaphysically inevitable in love, as defined by the high level of the two central characters, as the main element in the central idea of the play, then it is. Then this tragedy contains something apocalyptic.

It is fortunate that Shakespeare did not pre-plan the illustration of an idea. He relied on a story that was believed to be true at the time, but which had legendary dimensions. He took it from a naïve narrative poem, and in accordance with his method, dramatized it, heightening its incidents. He did not think about us, as a contemporary playwright would have. Nor did he state his idea explicitly, or bury it under allegories. He let the story speak effortlessly in its own tongue, freely.

That is why it says a lot. That is why we are allowed to philosophize about it, as we do about a piece of real life. The idea of the unattainable in love, suggested to us in this way, belongs equally to us and to the story. To the story because it formulates a defining element, a *moira* of its heroes. To us, because it requires our active participation and interpretation, so that it can be brought into the light.

The absolute calls for death as its necessary outcome. We know this from other tragedies too — from all tragedies. The revealing element, however, especially in *Romeo and Juliet*, is the suspicion that there exists a hidden relation, not a well-balanced antithesis in the love-death diptych. Love, thus, appears as an ontologically tragic condition. It ceases to be the mechanical perpetuator of suffering, but through suffering, it becomes the tragic savior.

IX

Bloodstained Freedom

THE MANNER in which we began this essay demanded a raw language, which does not shy away from the repugnant, just as it cannot be restrained by the so common prejudice of an established, "absolving" optimism. We should not think that the love motif, although excessively used in the dramaturgy of the contemporary world, has been fully explored, even when it happens to attain the tragic depth that lies beyond dramatic production. In our discussion of Shakespeare's *Romeo and Juliet*, we hinted at some of the innate tragic aspects of love. They are not the only ones. Kierkegaard in his *Treatise on Despair* makes a very crucial observation that as yet has only indirectly found its application in dramatic poetry. Here is what is pertinent: Even the most beautiful and most lovable thing that exists for man — femininity in the flower of its youth, full of calmness, harmony, and joy — is despair. And happiness, certainly; but does happiness constitute a category of the spirit? Not at all. For in its depths, in the most secret recesses of happiness dwells anguish also, which is despair, which seeks nothing more than to remain hidden; because despair longs for nothing more than a place in the remotest depths of happiness.

This observation of the Danish philosopher, which will certainly astonish the complacent, touches the very heart of the problem. Is this perhaps another aspect of the "absolute" that we hinted at in speaking about *Romeo and Juliet*? The undetermined yearning (not the sensual one, which the girl-child in full blossom awakens with her presence) is not merely thirst and anguish for something unattainable that transcends our existence. It is also an irrational affliction, as if from an elliptical revelation: an invitation to initiation, a possibility of euphoria — but never a fulfillment. In the very nature of beauty there is an inviolable code — an unquenched thirst. There is nothing more mysterious than the beautiful as it manifests itself in the human being. All other phenomena of the world, and the responses that they find in us, have a more or less rational explanation. Beauty has none. The more we try to define it, the more we find it dissolving into abstract, bloodless words. The beautiful girl entices us and makes us shudder — this is all that can be said.

Not even the girl herself, the bearer of the mystery, can explain it. She is not conscious of it; she merely bears it. And the less conscious of it she is, the more authentic she is. The question therefore concerns a symbol; revealing what truth? We do not know. Beauty is symbol, not allegory.

If you sleep with the girl-child symbol, if you submit her to the bondage of the flesh, you will inevitably fall victim to a deception. You will think that you have conquered something, made it your own — which is deceptive, and thus elusive. Or you will realize that "it was not that," but something else, unattainable. And, indeed, it was something else. Beauty only beckoned to you, did not stay for you to usurp it. No one can usurp it. It permitted you to pass it by without touching its essence. You touched it only superficially, like an arrow flying through the air, vanishing into the void, missing the target. That is why satiety, habit, boredom, disappointment, misunderstanding, all these by-products and "disclosures" that accompany the cohabitation of human beings, have no bearing on the true object of love. The target, imperceptibly, becomes transposed. We grow weary of something different from what we have loved. The former vanished as soon as it had beckoned to us, at an inconceivable and unrepeatable moment. In love, the person appears consumed by a strange purpose. And this contributes to the feeling of the tragic, which is an intuition, not knowledge.

In this essay I do not wish to give a spectacular place to love. I am not carried away by a trend in the contemporary world that often begins with a demagogic expediency: an easily likable, picturesque lyricism, or scandal that taints the theme of love. I am not concerned with the notion that the preferences of all men automatically converge at this point. But I divine in love an elemental force containing both the ancient and the contemporaneous, the blood and the mystery, deception and desire, the murderous and the sacred, the reflection of a beginning and the shadow of the end — all these tied together in a knot, an enigma. When one says this, one also says "tragedy." Because one has now sunk to the existential root, to the immemorial and inexplicable, to what existed before conscious life. Let us note that the ancient tragic poet, if he does not wear himself out as contemporary playwrights do on the theme of love as stage representation, always presupposes love in his outcome. And how intensely, how boldly! It is Clytemnestra's sinful bond to Aegisthus; the gadfly tormenting Io; the ancestral sins of the Labdakids; Deianira's and Medea's jealousy; Phaedra's inner wound; Electra's dark thirst nurturing revenge in her bowels like a lawless embryo. It is the sacred frenzy spurring the Bacchae. Always behind ancient Greek tragedy appears the specter of a panicked womb. And when you do not see it throbbing behind the proscenium, it is sung, mythicized by the Chorus in endless reveries about relationships and unions with the gods that bring forth traditions, initiate visions, mold legends, give light to heroes or monsters, weave a wisdom of life, the phantasmagoria of the incomprehensible which the world is.

In the tragedy of Romeo and Juliet we had the idyll. In *Antony and Cleopatra* we have the consuming erotic flame of twilight. In the first play the poet projected purity and unconsciousness as the main traits of love. In the second, sin. Not sin in the religious context, but a sin of situations, caused by voluntary relationships: adultery, jealousy, antagonism for the same person, or similar things. Sin in *Antony and Cleopatra* is organic, something destructive a priori, like a wrathful natural force. Here, it uproots characters, opposes history, the order of the organized world, the belief in a mission. Mark Antony undoes what he achieved in *Julius Caesar*: he betrays himself. His is the egotistic, passionate love of mature men, a barren love, not purified by fresh spontaneity from a youthful source. Love-debauchery, love the destroyer. The sacrificial sacredness of the erotic night that united the two children of Verona is undone here by Alexandrian orgies.

Shakespeare sees his Cleopatra as exotic; he playfully

confuses the Egyptian with the gypsy (words with the same etymology) in his imagination and portrays the daughter of the Ptolemies as swarthy, a gypsy. He calls her a "gipsy" with a heavily perfumed, sinful body, coiling slyly, like a dragon. The heroine's character, unstable, fluid, enchantingly unfaithful and treacherous, is not irrelevant to this image. And it is stressed that Cleopatra is of a mature age, so as to increase the density of the distilled venom congealed in her, a drug invincibly death-bearing.

> POMPEY: . . . *But all the charms of love,*
> *Salt Cleopatra, soften thy wan'd lip!*
> (II, i, 20–21)
>
> ANTONY: *You were half blasted ere I knew you . . .*
> (III, xi, 105)

Daring, crafty, artful, womanly with legendary significance, wily, deft in love, hard-hearted, lascivious, Cleopatra creates an unforgettable figure of personified sin — if sin we can call an invincibly destructive power. She is diametrically opposite to Juliet, who had the secret premonition of the sacred. And in the damned nature of Cleopatra lies enough grandeur to ensure her not only royal dignity, not only tragic pathos, but also the trait that makes her ravishing like a natural force. She has the enchantment of death.

Opposite this "eternal" woman, Antony is portrayed as huge. That is how he is announced in Philo's first words. He is explosive. No one knows what magnifies him more: his virtues or his faults. Or a synthesis of them. But what synthesis? The secret lies in this balance. Built of monumental dimensions, he represents the male legend just as Cleopatra embodies the female legend. In this respect they both are akin; they were created to meet: they fill the world. That is why their personal history transcends history, unsettles it with the power of myth; because in their entanglement is expressed again an archetypal pattern — only in a different meaning from that of Romeo and Juliet. If one wishes to examine this more closely, one will see that the contribution of Shakespeare, who otherwise has followed Plutarch, consists precisely in this. It is conclusive. Behind history, the poet has diagnosed the potentiality of the legend, whence he has molded and secured it for the centuries. Without Shakespeare, the entanglement of Antony and Cleopatra would be an academic question. Thanks to him, it became a tragedy, definitive as a seal stone.

Now one senses why the play appears chaotic, why it seems to lack condensed economy. This is its essential quality. The text annoys us because it does not fit on our stage, as if it had been written for it! Space and time in the tragedy of Antony and Cleopatra are trampled freely; the stage is the world. Around the action breathes the whole earth (and in this Shakespeare must have been helped by the medieval Mysteries, with their cosmological stage conception). The width of the platform is boundless, just as the brilliancy of the whole is dazzling. The action follows the fluctuations of a storm, the swirls of enraged wind. It is annihilating passion in conflict with history, or rather the individuals who take on a stature that renders them capable of counterbalancing the anonymous whole, traditionally the foundation of history.

Another question arises here — unanswerable, just like those which tragedy poses and excites: With whom does justice lie? With the two sinners who captivate us, or with the enemy camp, which will win in the end, but whose justification bears no relation to aesthetic emotion? The secret law of tragedy is aesthetic, not ethical, and here it appears as if we touch upon a fundamental antinomy pointing to something fearful; a state within a state, where beauty can be sinful even, or damned, with its inherent laws irrelevant to ethics, if not contrary to them. It is revealed to us now like another universe, where different laws are in force, compelling us to search for strange, artificial equilibria in order to conciliate the ethical with the beautiful, the practical needs of daily life with our lascivious thirst for admiration. Oedipus: sinful, yet more beautiful than Creon; Antigone: disobedient, yet lofty in character; Brutus and Cassius: guilty of homicide, yet moving; Faustus: blasphemous, yet shuddering; Juliet: insubordinate, yet invincible. Antony and Cleopatra are sinners – and they are great for this reason. If in fact we look for extreme examples — Richard III, Macbeth — then the confusion becomes more intense and at the same time the clarity more striking: In tragedy a secret law in us, more primitive than ethical law, demands satisfaction.

Antony's love for Cleopatra is a degrading love (see the entire end of Act III, after the escape from Actium, viii) suggesting, as retribution, the heroic despair of the final flame (Act IV, ii) which recalls Macbeth; and the superb vigor of the entire Act IV, iv:

> ANTONY. *Eros! Mine armour, Eros!*
>
> (IV, iv, 1)

It is not accidental that otherwise simple words suddenly attain proverbial significance. Innate and preeminently historical events allude to this. Antony's stature is essential to tragedy. Within these boundaries only death is comparable; because death is the absolute, the leap beyond the bondage of life, the transcendence of the ultimate limit determined by self-preservation, which is the standard of the masses. Even long before death, grandeur is established by the consciousness of tragic deception:

> ANTONY: *You have been a boggler ever:*
> *But when we in our viciousness grow hard —*
> *O misery on't! — the wise gods seel our eyes*
> *In our own filth drop our clear judgements, make us*
> *Adore our errors; laugh at's while we strut*
> *To our confusion.*
>
> (III, xi, 110–115)

I will not devote the space to the tragedy of Antony and Cleopatra that I have to other earlier tragedies, because it has already yielded to us all we need for our harvest. And now it is time to gather up this harvest.

I explained at the start that the intent of this essay was not to exhaust the subject or the particular forms of the tragic. It has attempted a free inquiry, subjective to some extent, aiming at revealing essential traits of tragedy. Occasionally it has wished to feel the pulse of the tragic, to experience and designate something of the tragic shiver. In the final analysis, this author wonders again, after all his wandering, if such a vibration can be made public. But we human beings are created this way: we thirst for communication; we live for sharing with each other. In our involvement in the social structure, or even in the anchorite withdrawal — in the two extremes, that is — this is what we always seek: communication with our fellow man — or with God, even when we deny him. We live for dialogue. The passion for dialogue — a dialogue which is not always consequential, yet when its consequence reaches our ears remains inexplicable — this is the spirit of tragedy.

Of the questions we have touched upon in midcourse, there is one that we do not have the right to overlook. It is predestination. This is closely related to the essence of tragedy, because it suggests two of its concordant notes: self-determinism and responsibility. Let us then try once more to proceed through this thorny realm. First of all, there is a religious point of view in this question, and a philosophical one. We state from the start that we can follow neither. The religious point of view is interrelated with the dogma of Divine Grace, and this leads us outside the universe of tragedy. It is faith that becomes the spokesman thereafter, not the sense of the tragic. Again, the philosophical point of view moves unquestioningly in the sphere of abstract concepts; but tragedy refers to the sphere of life experience. The tragic is a profound life experience, but in no case whatsoever can it find its restitution in the realm of the abstract. The divergence between life experience and the abstract is apparent in a simple instance of everyday life, in the fact that the latter can never cure the former: We philosophize and yet we suffer; we suffer and yet we philosophize. Tragic thought does not aspire to remedy the tragic.

We left Mark Antony at his fall, at an error-struck catastrophe. His error arose from his idiosyncrasy; this is why Mark Anthony became a person of tragedy in his own play and not in *Julius Caesar*, where he appeared invincible. In *Julius Caesar* Antony's mission was functional; in his own tragedy it is organic. Our tragic hero is then presented to us as marked.

Marked is Oedipus, marked is Faustus, marked are Phae-

dra and Hippolytus, Romeo and Juliet, Antony and Cleopatra. And we could add to this list — not to give the
impression that we have chosen examples in support of our
argument — Orestes and Hamlet, Antigone and Othello,
Medea and Macbeth, Ajax and Lear, the two Richards.

And now the question that arises is a relentless "why?"
A secret design seems to determine Oedipus' life. His example was useful, and we examined it first, because in its
entanglement of the three oracles it declares what is only
latent in the other tragedies. We can wonder whether
indeed a Necessity dictates Romeo's meeting with Juliet,
the coincidence that Iago is Othello's standard-bearer,
Macbeth's union with his lady. We cannot wonder why
Oedipus should meet Laius at the triple crossroads of
Daulis or why the Thebans offered him Jocasta as his
prize. A higher will has ordained it so, and we are merely
told of it. The hero, as we have noted, appears ensnared
from birth. Here predestination appears with a boldly un-
covered face.

We agree. But does not absolute predestination automatically abolish free will? And does not the negation of
free will mean the abolition of every notion of responsibility? The correlation of these syllogisms is implacable.
Thus the dilemma is clearly expressed: In tragedy are the
heroes condemned a priori, like puppets with only seeming
freedom? Or are the heroes free and responsible persons,
so that predestination is a deception, something like a
mirage, like a projection on a screen before the drama of
a man who will only be shaped during the action and by
the action?

Is what appears as Necessity perhaps a typical result of
the action? Or is it a consequence of the challenge unconsciously addressed by a human existence, merely be-

cause it exists? To whom? We do not know. Here is
another formulation of the question, with the virtue of
bringing us closer to the poetic reality of tragedy. What
new element has been added to this proposition? The contribution of the tragic hero. An impersonal contribution
anyway, for there is no mention yet of "character," but
only of an inert existence. If we accept Heracleitus' "Character is man's destiny," then the problem, like the Gordian
knot, is solved with one ax-blow. Initiative and responsibility, everything, are undertaken by the character. A
deceptive solution. Because the problem is only transposed: instead of asking about action, we will ask about
character. If the character is responsible for his actions,
then who is responsible for the character?

Established justice stops here. It does not search before
or beyond character, which it considers the first cause,
charging it with responsibility and imposing the penalty.
Because established justice is concerned with law-abiding
order and its preservation, it serves a practical expediency.
At best it might seek leniency allowing for the accidental
or innate, a confusion of mind or an organic injury. This
function is in fact mechanical: it is regulated proportion-
ately by the magnitude of the penalty. In tragedy, though,
what is tested is our psychic equilibrium, and beyond it,
even deeper, our attitude toward the phenomenon of life·
Shall we consider ourselves its child or its victim? Tragedy
then is a "paradigm," just as Oedipus was a "paradigm" -
the ancient poet's word now acquires a more essential
meaning.

At this point, a new distinction is imposed upon us by
the events themselves: the sense of necessity according to
the ancient consciousness vs. the sense of necessity according to the modern consciousness. In the universe of the

ancient world, Necessity attains a metaphysical dimension; it is the inexplorable whether or not it has been mythicized. Necessity and *Dike* appear as daughters of primeval Kronos; they are roots sunk into the very First Beginning. Necessity is the Mother of the Fates, as Plato would have it. Necessity is a dreadful deity, with her sanctuary inviolate, according to Pausanias, for no one has the right to set foot in it. All these point to a resignation in the ancient soul, an avoidance of advancing further. The feeling of ancient mystery once again is obvious here. The inexplorable is not guarded by prohibition, but by reverence.

For us, necessity has a mechanical, causal structure. Let us say so at once, so as not to lose ourselves in pointless discourse. Even for us the necessity of tragedy is not that. Logically, after a performance we can sit down and contemplate whether a character's essential elements are biological, hereditary, pathological, or sociological. We can contemplate whether we should search for the very source of actions in this tangle. Poetically — and the effect of tragedy is exclusively poetic — there is no place for an analysis of this kind. In the theater we function directly, psychically; we answer with a response, not with a noninvolved, cold judgment. In tragedy then, even today, necessity appears somewhat as it did for the ancient spectator. Hamlet's character does not put the key in our hands nor do the young prince's family entanglements, which are independent of his will. Hamlet's character is just as necessary for the revelation of the tragic as the myth that sets it into motion. If we consider the former as a definitive answer to the latter — that is, the turn the latter takes — the entire tragedy would be superfluous, and it would be equivalent — we sense this at once — to juggling: we would solve the mystery of the tragic with the abolition of tragedy.

We thus see something unexpected happening. Even for us — in spite of what has been said — tragedy, rightly understood and rightly performed, contains sanctity. Sanctity is this: the feeling of potential mystery. The recognition that there exists one realm of reason, and also another realm where logic is not only ineffective but becomes noisome even, indiscreet, something with a different name. It seems as if we need more of the irrational than our mere encounters with it in the external world. The irrational exists because we need it. And because we need it, many of us admit it exists. The logical coherence of this syllogism is not indisputable, due to the fact that it concerns a fictitious syllogism automatically placed outside the inherent laws of reason. Therefore, it is a proposition assuming the syllogistic method. We act in bad faith if we try to apply the laws of one universe to another that is diametrically opposite. In bad faith and with the rigidity of intellectual totalitarianism. That is why such irreconcilability has its absolute power in our organically totalitarian era, an era which has found a way to make even democracy totalitarian.

Tragedy, as in the past and always, presents to us a mythologized necessity. Predestination, if it is projected as a "paradigm" in Oedipus' life, is the predestination of humankind, not of the individual. That is why the story of Laius' son finds such a general response, beyond its external peculiarity. Whose life is not predestined if we examine it from the end to the beginning? The oracle is this retrospective glance, the advance pay-off of a posteriori wisdom. The oracle is the transcendence of the linear and therefore conventional course of Time. Since we do not know our future, we think it is alien to every other design. Would we have the same impression if it were possible to see the course of events all at once, as something completed and not as a contingency? Because such a contingency, most simply, would not be the future.

Predestination in certain exceptional cases resembles a scandal. What differentiates these from other predestinations, predestination in general, is prediction, the oracle — not fate, harsh or kind. From the moment that one prophecy existed, all prophecies could exist. What is accidental is not that one oracle was pronounced, but that all oracles are not pronounced for all destinies.

If I exclude character from predestination, the "self" that remains is purely fictitious. *I* am my character, the person thinking in this way or that, who has peculiar dispositions, intentions, tendencies, notions. These ancestors. This style of life. If I transfer *moira* to character, even the last line of fortification differentiating me from the external world, the world of phenomena, will collapse. The self then becomes an abstraction. Since I alone shape events and reactions, the external world is transformed into an obscure given. I live in an insubstantial world. And then I suddenly see where this poetic solipsism leads: to my becoming insubstantial myself! Because nothing can exist in nothingness. The absolute negates the relative.

Conventionally, to ensure the tragic hero's responsibility, we need to consider his will free. Our refusal, however, to assent to prosaic thinking, to convention, is useless, for with the acceptance of predestination the merit of responsibility collapses. Here we have the most contested point. Let us say at once that tragedy does not give a categorical answer to this question. And since tragedy as action does not give such an answer, we have no right to give one on its behalf. What can we do? Record its will faithfully. And then, when we have done so, we see something unexpected emerging.

The problem of metaphysical freedom, we see, is inherently essential to the tragic. We say "problem," and this means what cannot be surmised, but what is posed. Tragedy is the drama of metaphysical freedom. The word "drama" here takes many meanings. Berdyaev has seen rightly, very deeply, when he says that the truest tragedy is the tragedy of freedom and not of fact. The tragedy of freedom equals the *problem* of freedom, a tormenting question. When the question is directed to a level above our heads, higher than the level of laws, of institutions, and mores, then we cross over into the category of the tragic. Freedom, says Kierkegaard, is the dialectics of the two categories: the possible and the necessary. The possible, that is free will; the necessary, that is the problem of free will.

If the problem of free will were solved, tragedy would not exist. It is not accidental that *Oedipus Tyrannus* leaves behind it a question — that of responsibility, in the case of an expressly stated predestination. *Julius Caesar* does the same, and *King Lear*, and every genuine tragedy. Only the formulation changes each time; the question, never. The genuine, the austere pathos in which the tragic hero breathes is due to this: to our secret anxiety that without his knowing it, a deception lies in ambush for him. A deeper illusion, suggested by the myth, other than the one that is purely circumstantial. An illusion that he is free, independent; an illusion that he has the potential to fight back; an illusion that he comes into conflict with realities; an illusion that he exists.

Tragedy has reached a boundary where values, that is,

realities, conflict, yet where secretly everything is disputed from the metaphysical point of view. When we are conscious of this, then we are left breathless — and this means that the tragic function has been fulfilled.

Have we then arrived at a definition? No. At an impression only. If tragedy is the drama of metaphysical freedom, let us consider, as we have said, the word "drama" as both a morphological specification and an existential pronouncement. It is something that contains action and is an ontological involvement. We may also add the meaning that the word drama has vaguely, but often, in everyday language: An indirect question, to an unknown recipient. A question posed through action and the anguish of involvement; that is the content of the term. When we perceive tragedy in this way, we will stop asking it practical questions, naïve, pointless, and indiscreet, brought to bear upon it from other spheres. We shall live tragedy, rather than interrogate it. Today we are interrogating it more than we are living it. This is only natural: we live in an age of inquisition.

And this is one of the reasons we no longer write tragedies. Nietzsche was right.

The reader must have noticed that this book has chosen its examples — plays and characters — from a very narrow circle: five tragic poets and two eras. In fact, I consider tragedy an exception, not a rule. It is not a dramatic genre cultivated at will, in every era. It is not a fruit of philological ambition. It is not a genre susceptible to all historical conditions.

From the typically recognized tragic poets of the history of the theater, I have omitted Racine, but not out of negligence. Racine officially introduces the type of poet (it existed even before him, but unofficially) who *wants* to

write tragedies; a type which will later increase marvel-
ously, down to our present day. Racine's characters are
ladies and gentlemen of high society, his plays are dramas
in verse, brilliantly constructed, well-balanced, but not
tragedies. With them we enter the artificially scented
world of the salon. There is nothing pure in the faces of
these heroes, nothing wild and primitive out of the tragic,
hence cosmological world — nothing in their ambience
out of the strong scent of the forest and the stream of
blood. The *fureurs* of the French Phaedra are the wailings
of a courtly lady who knows how to beautify her orgasm
in lovely alexandrines. Its poet writes exquisite verses for
the ear, which aspire strenuously to become tragic, in
order actually to be so.

I certainly do not intend to dismiss Racine, a genuinely
great poet, with these few concluding remarks. Nor can
they impair his reputation. I only explain why I have not
drawn any examples from his works. And I pause at a
characteristic point in *Phèdre* as evidence.

Racine's Hippolyte does not yield to his stepmother's
erotic advances, not only because a guilty relationship
with her frightens him, not only because he is irrevocably
devoted to Artemis, the grimly virginal goddess, not only
because he comes from another dissimilar world, as Euripides' hero does, but because he is in love with someone
else: Aricie. The untamed wild beast of the woods has
become in Racine's hands a *jeune premier*, a courtier
longed for by both girls and married women. He flirts,
wastes himself in elegant speech, pays elaborate compli-
ments to the ladies, utters limpid expressions ("Présente je
vous fuis, absente je vous trouve"), has charming eloquence. It is obvious that he intoxicates the women with
his words. One of our contemporary critics who greatly
favors Racine, George Steiner (and I have chosen him pur-

posely, a non-Frenchman, unaffected by chauvinism, or even by his educational background), explains in his famous book *The Death of Tragedy:* "the image of a royal prince fleeing at the approach of women would have struck the contemporary audience as ridiculous." But this explains exactly why in the years of Louis XIV no tragedy could have been written. A world that needs such ridiculous social conventions in order to become interested in lofty drama, and which measures the forms of myth with its daily mores, is by definition alien to the tragic. An Hippolyte in love is no longer Hippolytus. We have entered the territory of bedroom drama. A Phèdre angered at her inner storm because of an ordinary jealousy is no longer the daughter of Minos and Pasiphaë, despite Racine's legendary, virtually enchanting lines — but only the lines, not their content, claim so. Diction now functions independently of the tragic myth, an end in itself, which seeks pleasure through itself. This is the crucial breach. On one hand the tragic, on the other the florid style.

But look at the consequence. No one believes even for a moment in what these characters say. They are subject to an involuntary "remoteness," a misfortune of the worst sort in the theater. They are masked courtiers assembled to give an amateur performance and entertain their master. They talk about altars, sanctuaries, mythological deities, and you sense the courtiers of the period in their thick wigs. Masked snobs, thinking they perform tragedy, whereas they perform their amateurism. Steiner mentions as suggestive of the ancient demonic world, Hippolyte's quatrain:

> *Les monstres étouffés et les brigands punis,*
> *Procruste, Cercyon, et Scyrron, et Sinnis,*

Et les os disperses du géant d'Epidaure,
Et la Crète fumant du sang du Minotaure.

(I, i, 79–82)

But this is an exemplary exercise in rhetoric or a refrain from the libretto of a melodrama. It has the virtue of not needing musical accompaniment, because it contains it. But this is all. We are in the realm "thrice removed from the truth."
Another symptom:

La détestable Oenone a conduit tout le reste.

(V, vii, 32)

The peak of cowardice! To rescue the honor of the aristocracy, they charge the ill-fated attendant with the responsibility of the sin. Because this woman belongs to a lower class, she will pay for the blunders of the great. The manner of thinking and the mores of typical high-caste persons, that is, of anti-tragic persons, fearful of responsibility. In this, Racine involuntarily reveals himself as an impeccable realist.

I do not know whether what Steiner has also observed is totally insignificant: that Racine did not have an innate love for the theater. Is the gloomy Jansenism of his childhood upbringing perhaps to blame?

"Racine was a court poet," Steiner writes explicitly, "who accepted the caste values of his milieu. He worked for the stage, but not with it ... Racine is one of those great dramatic poets (Byron was another) who had no natural liking for the theatre." But Byron was never counted among the assets of the theater. The comparison is condemnatory. On the one hand Racine, a great poet to be sure, but one who did not like the theater, and on the other a society fundamentally anti-tragic (which found its pure dimensions only in Molière's satire) managed — according to the history of the theater — to create tragedy. One marvels — and wonders. Racine's example is precious, because it clarifies something more than we had initially asked of him. This shows the historicity of tragedy. It is the fruit of exceptional conditions that appear under extremely rare and unforeseen circumstances.

Steiner's example makes me think many times that — I say perhaps — men like him, really talented otherwise, have not been able to surmise the essence of Attic tragedy because they have been acquainted with it only through translations, that is, in an unrecognizable form. They have never received the holy communion with its body and its blood. Otherwise such mistakes cannot be explained. In Racine's case, neither the poet nor his critic have understood that tragedy is of a prerational kind. Steiner praises indirectly Racine's assertion in the preface to his *Iphigénie*, "that reason and good sense are the same in all centuries," and that "Parisian taste showed itself to be in accord with that of Athens."

When both poet and critic set out from such ground how can they reach a place where we can meet them?

We end where we started: tragedy cannot be born of good will. It is a hidden ore, molded in the depths of some very old geological stratum by a secret process. It emits a radiance that is not of the surface world, a black light.

We should consider ourselves exceptionally fortunate when we are able to approach and experience it. As for re-creating it, if this were to happen, we would not have sought it. Here Pascal's words are valid in reverse: "You would not have sought me if you had not found me." It

is not possible to reach tragedy; that is why we seek it passionately, agitated by apprehension and anxiety lest we be
left short.

Of what? Of tragic reality? No. Of tragic ambition?
Not that either — but of tragic grandeur. Of the belief
that man has a fourth dimension, which the universe
denies him.

X

The Tragic Age

Thou shouldst not have been old till thou hadst been wise
— King Lear, (I, v, 45)

THIS FOURTH DIMENSION is made perceptible by the tragic age.

For there exists an age of tragedy. It is youth. I will say here why and how, but first I must explain this assertion, although I believe, intuitively at least, that it is self-evident for each of us.

Tragedy equals the age of magnanimity, of bountiful offering. Just as we consider inconceivable a stingy tragic hero (the miser creates comedy — Molière has proven this: Shylock is not a miser, he serves the passion of wounded selfishness; that is why, when wrongly interpreted, he shifts the balance to comedy — Shakespeare has proven this); therefore, the more stinginess is incompatible with tragedy, the more generosity is compatible with it. More than this: it is one of its essential elements. It is precisely because of their generosity that all tragic heroes are young without exception, regardless of their age, starting with the oldest, King Lear. Any discussion of the younger ones — Orestes, Hamlet, Antigone, or Iphigenia — is unnecessary; they arc children of prodigality. There is something childlike about all of them, without exception. Only when they attain it — if they did not have it initially — do they become worthy of being tragic heroes. Mark Antony did not have it in *Julius Caesar*, that is why he was not tragic; he was politically effective. He acquires it later, as the victim of Cleopatra, and then he becomes worthy of a tragedy of his own.

With this generosity is associated a strange naïveté, again a trait of childlikeness. These two are concurrent in any case. Philoctetes and Brutus, Ajax and Othello, Prometheus and Faustus appear naïve to us. Even when their naïveté is not plastically projected, as an idiosyncratic trait, it is suggested by the world that contains them. Hamlet is cunning (in some way), but his ideas have a fresh naïveté, as does his innocence. An old or aged world, a world wrinkled by some deficiency, can neither believe in tragic myths nor accept tragic heroes. It calls tragic heroes the victims of unexpected misfortune. Today we live in a wrinkled world that schemes a lot, and is artfully sinful, that is, indulges in ruminating about its feelings of guilt. We have escaped from a fear of damnation after death without relieving ourselves of the sense of sin. We are sinners before a god we have obliterated. We have obliterated God — but his law has remained, like a bee's sting in the flesh.

Youth is the age of generosity; it is also the age of epic. Here epic and tragedy meet. Both are manifestations of the same moment, based on psychic abundance. He who is capable of becoming an epic hero can also become a hero of tragedy. Prometheus drags an epic behind him like a purple robe; as does Philoctetes, as well as Eteocles, Orestes, Faustus, Othello, Richard III, and Macbeth. The vast breath that forms the waves in epic also produces the storm with tragedy's thunderbolt. All this should be taken seriously, otherwise we cannot enter the tragic universe. We cannot enter the tragic universe with the stinginess of skepticism, the mockery of iconoclastic nihilism, the dissolvingly critical thought. We enter the tragic realm innocent, with confidence and an open stride.

Physiologically, youth's inspiration is aroused by sexual euphoria, by the mission for perpetuation. Unknown to us, something has been entrusted to youth that creates, one way or another, an inner climate. This entails daring, a pioneering spirit — and at the beginning we saw that the pioneer spirit was essential to the tragic spirit. No tragedy can be created with *sophrosyne* (self-control, prudence). *Sophrosyne* is a delaying force; it is also the restorer that returns order after the tragic hero has been crushed. In one sense, one could say that tragedy means a conflict between the pioneer spirit and *sophrosyne*. Ultimately the Greek tragic poets proclaim *sophrosyne*, but after they have first allowed their tragic hero to realize his starry epic. Strange, indeed, is this balance in ancient tragedy: on the one hand it extols sin, hubris, and on the other preaches *sophrosyne*. But the ancient tragic poets seem to speak for *sophrosyne* in order to keep in line with established morality, with the omnipotent general feeling, as well as to inform the mediocre — those incapable of ascending the tragic peaks where the irreparable prevails. The tragic hero stands as an exception, and on this his redeeming grace relies, and his nobility as well — a nobility innate to his character and very dearly paid for — therefore unrepeatable. We envy him, but without malice. The Greek tragic poets speak ultimately for *sophrosyne*, because they believe that it is the measure that the gods have granted men for their use. It is what every totalitarian regime employs. The gods demand obeisance; the tragic hero is a rebel. Within the ancient tragic poet, admiration for the hero and fear of the gods conflict; consequently, the obvious voice, the second, prevails over the first. Thus tragedy ends up being the entity that contains a hidden admiration and a manifest conformation. It is a secret entity. Conflict appears in the tragic poet's soul itself; he himself seems to contain the pioneer spirit, the daring of a tightrope walker. His connection, however, with society and with the duty of citizenship imposes upon him a pious conformation. Tragedy is the secret, allegorical representation of the poet's imaginary sin.

Genetic élan, as we saw it when we discussed the love tragedies, has a tragic character: not only the utmost intensity, instantly rebuffed in attaining its personal target (the experience of the absolute), which *knows* it will be deceived both as begetter of mortal men and as perpetuator of suffering and personal death; but also a blind drive, leading to the extremes of total self-consummation and sometimes even murder. The erotic élan itself, in its climactic moment, is a symbolic murder, where both the one who stabs and the one who is stabbed writhe in mutual guilty pleasure. Hence, the secrecy of the erotic experience, its need for darkness, reticence, isolation, the indefinite feeling of sin that agitates pleasure. Lawfulness blunts pleasure, for it abolishes the mystery of sin.

Pleasure-absolute-youth-tragic seems to comprise a correlation that expresses, though in an indecipherable way, the enigma of being.

But why do we say that the fourth dimension is denied by the universe, since this fourth dimension is the tragic age? What is more in accord with the will of natural law than youth? If there exists an age that makes apparent, indeed celebrates, the will of the secret lawmaker, it is youth.

Here an explanation is necessary.

One of the missions with which the unknown commander has entrusted us, and the only one that is self-evident and in accord with the general rhythm of organic life, is perpetuation. This we have said already, and it is a commonplace. It is a blind mission, at least to the extent that its target is invisible, and the logic that designs it is incongruent with man's logic.

Youth, charged with this mechanical function, and well-endowed to serve it with elation, defends it with a passion that appears selfish, because it is inevitably identified with it. For this is always the demand of the natural world. The question, now, is not whether another world exists, metaphysical or transcendental — a futile question for an inquiry like ours. We will therefore limit ourselves to making the assumption that tragedy demonstrates the existence of a category representative of youth that is not identical with physiological youth.

The youth of the tragic hero, we have said, is his naïveté and his tender generosity even in sin or murder. These make him sacrifice his life recklessly, for a passion, or a cause, or an illusion. There is youth in this fervor, but a peculiar youth, which has only a few traits in common with the other, general and anonymous youth. Tragedy's youth is not an abstract idea of youth, nor of conventional age. It is a trait of the psyche, a seal of grace or damnation.

Thus, the tragic hero's youth at once transcends and encompasses his incidental age. Romeo, Juliet have the youth of tragedy, not the youth of ordinary life. They idealize the latter, thanks to the radiance of the former.

Every eighteen-year-old boy, every fourteen-year-old girl, is not a latent Romeo or Juliet. The legendary lovers of Verona have nothing in common with everyday children, except for the remote possibility that one may see among myriads of ordinary children one or two who recall, in a fleeting nuance, that pair. But this slightest link suffices. Youth is sanctified in the union of the lovers of Verona, because this union projects from within the limits of ordinary life what is supreme and unreachable.

There exists, therefore, in addition to physical youth, another youth: the ideal one; so ideal that it is irrelevant to other ages. The aims of this youth actually bear no relation to the commandment that Nature has entrusted to the tender age. Romeo and Juliet do not unite in order to bear children. Their love is self-contained. From the moment — as we have said — that we imagine them having many children, we descend unavoidably to the physical plane, and reduce them from their legend, believing that the children they will bear cannot possibly resemble them, cannot possibly repeat the legendary experiment. It was ideal, because it was unrepeatable. Romeo and Juliet's children must in one way or another be like other children of the world: beings who are only formally realized, just for an instant, because of their transient ages. But it would be a pity if we tried to see Romeo and Juliet through the exclusive prism of their age. More than age, they represent two exceptional natures. Let us say more precisely: two natures in full blossom *thanks* to their age. It is *age* that is glorified because of Romeo and Juliet, not Romeo and Juliet because of their age.

Thus, the tragic hero's youth manifests itself in a spiritual, not a boldly physiological form. What, then, makes us say "youth" and not simply naïveté and generosity, which are its most palpable ingredients? Something strangely matutinal is hidden in it: a powerful desire, although damned at times. Richard III slays his enemies with the cruelty of a child who dismembers flies, removing their wings and legs. But let us be fair: Richard is a wronged, crippled child, malformed from birth, physically maimed, and one feels that a proud sadness looms in the cellar of his sunless soul. An insidious crab with the disposition for metaphysical rebellion. He commits evil so impulsively that at times it appears unaccountable; at other times, with the satanism of a warped child taking revenge on his stepmother. For Nature has been a stepmother to Richard of Gloucester. The justification, here the dramatic, not moral justification, lies in his epic awareness of his intellectual superiority to an entire world: Richard is superior to all others in the play; he is the most worthy to reign; he takes, therefore, what belongs to him, only he takes it in an inhuman way, in the same way that he had been deprived, even before he was born, of common human grace. To counterbalance this, as if to reinforce his satanic dynamism, he has a radiance, a unique vivacity, finally a dark charm: he mesmerizes like the abyss. He is something between a warped child and a demon, a demon at a young age.

Medea's revenge also has a childlike cruelty, the blind and disproportionate cruelty of juvenile hysteria. Among the ancient heroes only Clytemnestra seems to me to be deprived of the bitter tenderness of the young assassins; but Clytemnestra is not a tragic heroine; the heroine of her tragedy (*Agamemnon*) is Cassandra; Electra, Orestes, and Iphigenia are heroes elsewhere.

Let us not elaborate upon this comparison; we needed it only for a certain reason. The youth that comes into conflict with the order of the universe is a symbolic youth. It represents the demand of certain beings to discover and impose a tablet inscribed with their own values upon an enormous mechanism that does not seem to have provided any reference to human values. The mechanism operates, crushing both the beings and their demands altogether. Afterward the question remains: what determines the mechanism? Some hidden moral order, or perhaps a vast indifference? In both instances, the decision to quarrel with the Unknown, with the inconceivable, presupposes a youthful recklessness.

Now that I have reached the end of this essay, I wish to reflect again on something that I kept thinking about as I wrote. Some readers will not fail to characterize the concept of tragedy that I maintain as "idealistic." I do not rebut this point of view because I consider it somewhat slanderous; each of us should have the courage of his beliefs. I will not mention that distinctions such as these seem to me rather unwieldly. I counter this characterization only to the extent necessary to clarify my real purpose.

The notion of the metaphysical (and very often we discovered metaphysical qualities in the plays we analyzed) seems at a first glance to be a letter without a recipient: on the one hand metaphysical expectations or illusions; on the other, a material, silent universe around us. As far as we are concerned, however, this is not the question. It is customary to link the metaphysical inclination in a closely causal connection with some unverified, transcendental order of things. This order, a transcendent world, seems to justify existence and reaffirm the metaphysical feeling.

This is wrong. The possible nonexistence of the transcendental does not negate human inner reality. The metaphysical emanates from us, and if it returns to us, this does not abolish its image. We are a small universe within another, unfathomable universe. Why at every step do we want to verify our values against its values? Because it has the power to contradict our values? But our life is annulled ultimately by the law of the universe; that is no reason to consider it insubstantial. We exist though we die, perhaps we exist in order to die. Death makes life worthy, creates for it an absolute measure. Our metaphysical anguish is also the silence of the universe.

In one sense tragedy may be the contact in a flash of lightning with some higher order of things; it may also be a futile search, an echoless cry vanishing in the chaos. It does not matter! The latter lays the foundation for tragedy no less than the former. Tragedy exists whether man believes he has discerned a distant, obscure response, or whether he awaits in vain the signal from afar, from within the mist that hides nothing.

Maybe man needs a certain boundary of naïveté in order to attempt such a dialogue. It is this boundary that we have called the tragic age. That is why it is defined by timelessness. King Lear grew old, but he did not become wise nor hollow, at least not before he was singed by the apocalypse of the law of ingratitude: "Thou shouldst not have been old till thou hadst been wise," his Fool tells him. Profound words! But if Lear had been wise, if he had been prudent, he would not have graced us with the gift of tragedy. Prudence gives birth to a low pedestrianism, and leaves the grave unjustified.

Sophrosyne is needed for the smoothest possible journey through life. But one can either be endowed with *sophrosyne,* or be a King Lear — king of the Myth. The crown of tragedy is bloodstained. It is worn by the great deceived ones of this world.

Notes

Notes

I. THE TRAGIC SPIRIT

Page
9 "Passion." θυμὸς δὲ κρείσσων τῶν ἐμῶν
βουλευμάτων . . .

18 "No mortal." οὔτις μερόπων ἀσινῆ βίοτον
διὰ παντὸς ἄτιμος ἀμείψει.

18 "Alas." ἰὼ γενεαὶ βροτῶν
ὡς ὑμᾶς ἴσα καὶ τὸ μη-
δὲν ζώσας ἐναριθμῶ.

19 "You." . . . σὺ σῶσον, σύ μ᾽ ἐλέησον, εἰσορῶν
ὡς πάντα δεινὰ κἀπικινδύνως βροτοῖς
κεῖται παθεῖν μὲν εὖ, παθεῖν δὲ θάτερα.
χρὴ δ᾽ ἐκτὸς ὄντα πημάτων τὰ δείν᾽ ὁρᾶν,
χὤταν τις εὖ ζῇ, τηνικαῦτα τὸν βίον
σκοπεῖν μάλιστα μὴ διαφθαρεὶς λάθῃ.

20 "But I do love thee." All quotations from Shakespeare are
according to *The Oxford Shakespeare* (New York: Oxford
University Press, n.d.)

23 "I yearn." ὁποῖα χρῄζει ῥηγνύτω· τοὐμὸν δ᾽ ἐγώ,
κεἰ σμικρόν ἐστι, σπέρμ᾽ ἰδεῖν βουλήσομαι.

II. SAVIOR DELIAN PAEAN!

32 Character fully developed. Bernard Knox, *Oedipus at Thebes* (New Haven: Yale University Press, 1957), p. 14. Paul Mazon holds the opposite view in the Prologue of the Belles Lettres edition of *Oedipus Tyrannus*.

34 Apostate. Nietzsche is the only one who understood this correctly.

38 Two or three altars. Most recent research has shown that such altars were standard scenographic accessories of the ancient theater. See G. M. Sifakis, *Studies in the History of the Hellenistic Drama* (London: University of London, Athlone Press, 1967), p. 51.

40 Ancients have remained very secretive. Parmenides is no exception to this. His poetic vision is a personal and philosophical allegory.

44 "Savior." ἰήιε Δάλιε Παιάν . . .

44 "Fear." . . . ἐκτέταμαι φοβερὰν φρένα
δείματι πάλλων,
ἰήιε Δάλιε Παιάν,
ἀμφὶ σοὶ ἀζόμενος τί μοι ἢ νέον
ἢ περιτελλομέναις ὥραις πάλιν
ἐξανύσεις χρέος.
εἰπέ μοι, ὦ χρυσέας τέκνον Ἐλπίδος,
ἄμβροτε Φάμα.

III. THE IMPURE ROOT AND THE
PERFECTLY PURE LIGHT—I

48 "Bow."   . . . ὁ δ'ἤιε νυκτὶ ἐοικώς.
ἕζετ' ἔπειτ' ἀπάνευθε νεῶν, μετὰ δ' ἰὸν ἕηκε·
δεινὴ δὲ κλαγγὴ γένετ' ἀργυρέοιο βιοῖο.

49 "Clearly, Lord."   ἄνωγεν ἡμᾶς Φοῖβος ἐμφανῶς ἄναξ
μίασμα χώρας, ὡς τεθραμμένον χθονὶ
ἐν τῆδ', ἐλαύνειν . . .

50 "Purification."   ποίῳ καθαρμῷ;

50 "Misfortune."   κακὸν δὲ ποῖον ἐμποδὼν τυραννίδος
οὕτω πεσούσης εἶργε τοῦτ' ἐξειδέναι;

51 "That enchanting."   ἡ ποικιλῳδὸς Σφὶγξ . . .

53 "O sweetly."   ὦ Διὸς ἀδνεπὲς φάτι, τίς ποτε . . .

54 "Proclaim."   τὸν ἄνδρ' ἀπαυδῶ τοῦτον, ὅστις ἐστί, γῆς
τῆσδ', ἧς ἐγὼ κράτη τε καὶ θρόνους νέμω,
μήτ' ἐσδέχεσθαι μήτε προσφωνεῖν τινά,
μήτ' ἐν θεῶν εὐχαῖσι μηδὲ θύμασιν
κοινὸν ποεῖσθαι, μήτε χέρνιβας νέμειν·
ὠθεῖν δ' ἀπ' οἴκων πάντας, ὡς μιάσματος
τοῦδ' ἡμὶν ὄντος, ὡς τὸ Πυθικὸν θεοῦ
μαντεῖον ἐξέφηνεν ἀρτίως ἐμοί.

55 "Those."   καὶ ταῦτα τοῖς μὴ δρῶσιν εὔχομαι θεοὺς
μήτ' ἄροτον αὐτοῖς γῆς ἀνιέναι τινὰ
μήτ' οὖν γυναικῶν παῖδας, ἀλλὰ τῷ πότμῳ
τῷ νῦν φθερεῖσθαι κἄτι τοῦδ' ἐχθίονι.

56 "Teiresias."   ὦ πάντα νωμῶν Τειρεσία, διδακτά τε
ἄρρητά τ' οὐράνιά τε καὶ χθονοστιβῆ . . .

57   "Apollo, Apollo."   Ἀπόλλων, Ἀπόλλων
ἀγυιᾶτ᾽, ἀπόλλων ἐμός·
ἀπολέσας γάρ οὐ μόλις τὸ δεύτερον.

57   "Apollo."   ἄναξ Ἄπολλον, ἵλεως αὐτοῖν κλύε
. . . .
νῦν δ᾽, ὦ Λύκει᾽ Ἄπολλον, ἐξ οἵων ἔχω
αἰτῶ, προπίτνω, λίσσομαι, γενοῦ πρόφρων
ἡμῖν ἀρωγὸς τῶνδε τῶν βουλευμάτων . . .

59   "This day."   ἥδ᾽ ἡμέρα φύσει σε καὶ διαφθερεῖ.

64   "Apollo."   Ἀπόλλων τάδ᾽ ἦν, Ἀπόλλων, φίλοι . . .

IV. THE IMPURE ROOT AND THE
PERFECTLY PURE LIGHT—II

67   "No mortal."   βρότειον οὐδὲν μαντικῆς ἔχον τέχνης.
. . . .
χρησμὸς γὰρ ἦλθε Λαΐῳ ποτ᾽, οὐκ ἐρῶ
Φοίβου γ᾽ ἀπ᾽ αὐτοῦ, τῶν δ᾽ ὑπηρετῶν ἄπο
. . . .
κἀνταῦθ᾽ Ἀπόλλων οὔτ᾽ ἐκεῖνον ἤνυσεν
φονέα γενέσθαι πατρὸς οὔτε Λάιον
τὸ δεινὸν οὑφοβεῖτο πρὸς παιδὸς παθεῖν.
. . . .
. . . ὧν γὰρ ἄν θεὸς
χρείαν ἐρευνᾷ ῥᾳδίως αὐτὸς φανεῖ.

68   "Just as I."   οἷόν μ᾽ ἀκούσαντ᾽ ἀρτίως ἔχει, γύναι,
ψυχῆς πλάνημα κἀνακίνησις φρενῶν.

68   "O Zeus."   ὦ Ζεῦ, τί μου δρᾶσαι βεβούλευσαι πέρι;

71   "Character."   ἀνθρώπῳ δαίμων.

75 "But whoever."   . . . ἀνδρῶν δ' ὅτι μάν-
τις πλέον ἢ 'γὼ φέρεται,
κρίσις οὐκ ἔστιν ἀληθής·
σοφίᾳ δ' ἂν σοφίαν
παραμείψειεν ἀνήρ.
ἀλλ' οὔποτ' ἔγωγ' ἄν,
πρὶν ἴδοιμ' ὀρθὸν ἔπος, μεμ-
φομένων ἂν καταφαίην.

76 "Alas, generations."   ἰὼ γενεαὶ βροτῶν,
ὡς ὑμᾶς ἴσα καὶ τὸ μη-
δὲν ζώσας ἐναριθμῶ.

. . . .
τὸν σόν τοι παράδειγμ' ἔχων,
τὸν σὸν δαίμονα, τὸν σόν, ὦ
τλᾶμον Οἰδιπόδα, βροτῶν
οὐδὲν μακαρίζω·

78 "Rain."   . . . μέλας
ὄμβρος χάλαζά θ' αἱματοῦσσ' ἐτέγγετο.

79 "He ran."   φωνῇ γὰρ ἡμᾶς ἔγχος ἐξαιτῶν πορεῖν,
γυναῖκά τ' οὐ γυναῖκα, μητρῷαν δ' ὅπου
κίχοι διπλῆν ἄρουραν οὗ τε καὶ τέκνων.

79 "Dreadfully."   . . . δεινὰ βρυχηθεὶς τάλας,
χαλᾷ κρεμαστὴν ἀρτάνην. ἐπεὶ δὲ γῇ
ἔκειτο τλήμων, δεινὰ δ' ἦν τἀνθένδ' ὁρᾶν.
ἀποσπάσας γὰρ εἱμάτων χρυσηλάτους
περόνας ἀπ' αὐτῆς, αἷσιν ἐξεστέλλετο . . .

79 "Many times."   . . . πολλάκις τε κοὐχ ἅπαξ

80 "O pure."   ὦ φάος ἁγνόν . . .

80 "O divine ether."   ὦ δῖος αἰθήρ . . .

81   "O light." ὦ φῶς, τελευταῖόν σε προσβλέψαιμι νῦν

83   "The union." James George Frazer, *The Golden Bough*
     (New York: The Macmillan Company, 1926), pp. 9–10.

V. An Everlasting Death

91   "Why wert." I feel sorry that the development of my
     argument, as presented here, presupposes some knowledge
     of the text; but how else could it be done? If we were to
     analyze thoroughly each work we need, we would arrive at
     different borderlines—and a different target.

101 Metaphysical   dimensions.   Each   revolution—Camus
     says—is metaphysical. He means, of course, revolutions,
     not uprisings.

VI. The Tragic Error

107 Objectively irrelevant. There is no absolute objectivity per
     se in a work of art. Jean Laplanche and J. B. Pontalis
     maintain in their *Vocabulaire de la psychanalyse* (edition
     P.U.P) "or if again, one accepts that a work of art has some
     meaning for its creator, this meaning should interest us no
     more than any other viewpoint."

VII. The Tragic Ecstasy

130 "Cypris." φοιτᾷ δ᾽ ἀν᾽ αἰθέρ᾽, ἔστι δ᾽ ἐν θαλασσίῳ
              κλύδωνι Κύπρις, πάντα δ᾽ ἐκ ταύτης ἔφυ·
              ἥδ᾽ ἐστὶν ἡ σπείρουσα καὶ διδοῦσ᾽ ἔρον,
              οὗ πάντες ἐσμὲν οἱ κατὰ χθόν᾽ ἔγγονοι.

131 "Those." ὅσοι μὲν οὖν γραφάς τε τῶν παλαιτέρων
              ἔχουσιν αὐτοί τ᾽ εἰσὶν ἐν μούσαις ἀεί,
              ἴσασι μὲν Ζεὺς ὥς ποτ᾽ ἠράσθη γάμων

Σεμέλης; ἴσασι δ᾽ ὡς ἀνήρπασέν ποτε
ἡ καλλιφεγγὴς Κέφαλον ἐς θεοὺς Ἕως
ἔρωτος εἴνεκ᾽· ἀλλ᾽ ὅμως ἐν οὐρανῷ
ναίουσι κοὺ φεύγουσιν ἐκποδὼν θεούς

131 "Eros." θέλγει δ᾽ Ἔρως, ᾧ μαινομένᾳ κραδίᾳ
            πτανὸς ἐφορμάσῃ χρυσοφαής,
            φύσιν ὀρεσκόων σκυλάκων πελαγίων θ᾽
            ὅσα τε γᾶ τρέφει
            τά τ᾽ ἀέλιος αἰθόμενα δέρκεται,
            ἄνδρας τε· συμπάντων βασιληίδα τιμάν,
            Κύπρι, τῶνδε μόνα κρατύνεις.

131 "Pleased." στέργουσι δ᾽, οἶμαι, ξυμφορᾷ νικώμενοι.

132 "Nothing." . . . οὐ γὰρ ἄλλο πλὴν ὕβρις
            τάδ᾽ ἐστί, κρείσσω δαιμόνων εἶναι θέλειν . .

132 "Cypris." . . . Κύπρις οὐκ ἄρ᾽ ἦν θεός,
            ἀλλ᾽ εἴ τι μεῖζον ἄλλο γίγνεται θεοῦ . . .

136 "Mother." ὦ τλῆμον, οἷον, μῆτερ, ἠράσθης ἔρον.

136 "And you." σύ τ᾽, ὦ τάλαιν᾽ ὅμαιμε, Διονύσου δάμαρ.

136 "And I." τρίτη δ᾽ ἐγὼ δύστηνος ὡς ἀπόλλυμαι

136 "But she." ἥ δ᾽ εἰς ἔλεγχον μὴ πέσῃ φοβουμένη
            ψευδεῖς γραφὰς ἔγραψε καὶ διώλεσεν
            δόλοισι σὺν παιδ᾽ . .

138 "He who chooses." αἰτία ἑλομένου· θεὸς ἀναίτιος.

138 "But if there." ἀλλ᾽ ὅ τι τοῦ ζῆν φίλτερον ἄλλο
            σκότος ἀμπίσχων κρύπτει νεφέλαις.
            τοῦ δ᾽ ὅ τι τοῦτο στίλβει κατὰ γῆν

δυσέρωτες δὴ φαινόμεθ᾽ ὄντες,
δι᾽ ἀπειροσύνην ἄλλου βιότου
κοὐκ ἀπόδειξιν τῶν ὑπὸ γαίας·
μύθοις δ᾽ ἄλλως φερόμεσθα.

139 "No god."   οὐδείς μ᾽ ἀρέσκει νυκτὶ θαυμαστὸς θεῶν.

139 "To your."   τὴν σὴν δὲ Κύπριν πόλλ᾽ ἐγὼ χείρειν λέγω.

139 "But."   ἢ δ᾽ εὐκλεὴς μέν, ἀλλ᾽ ὅμως ἀπόλλυται,
Φαίδρα· τὸ γὰρ τῆσδ᾽ οὐ προτιμήσω κακὸν
τὸ μὴ οὐ παρασχεῖν τοὺς ἐμοὺς ἐχθροὺς ἐμοὶ
δίκην τοσαύτην ὥστ᾽ ἐμοὶ καλῶς ἔχειν.

140 "Soothing philters."   . . . φίλτρα μοι θελκτήρια
ἔρωτος . . .

140 "Charms."   . . . ἐπῳδαὶ καὶ λόγοι θελκτήριοι . . .

140 "For if."   εἰ μὲν γὰρ ἦν σοι μὴ 'πὶ συμφοραῖς βίος
τοιαῖσδε, σώφρων δ᾽ οὖσ᾽ ἐτύγχανες γυνή,
οὐκ ἄν ποτ᾽ εὐνῆς οὕνεχ᾽ ἡδονῆς τε σῆς
προσῆγον ἄν σε δεῦρο· νῦν δ᾽ ἀγὼν μέγας
σῶσαι βίον σόν, κοὐκ ἐπίφθονον τόδε.

141 "I fear."   δέδοιχ᾽ ὅπως μοι μὴ λίαν φανῇς σοφή.

141 "Let that be."   ἔασον, ὦ παῖ . . .

VIII. BENEATH THE STAR OF DEATH

151 Absolute expression and balance. "A cry of blood which
tells us we have know them always," notes Gilbert Murray
in his essay "Hamlet and Orestes," in *The Classical Tradition in Poetry* (Cambridge: Harvard University Press,

1927), p. 239. Maud Bodkin in her book *Archetypal Patterns in Poetry* (London: Oxford University Press, 1934) focuses on this aspect of literary works which have left their mark through the passing of centuries.

156 "They are no more." Harley Granville-Barker, *Prefaces to Shakespeare*, V.2 (Princeton: Princeton University Press, 1951), p. 338.

163 Haunt nature. It is a shameful shunning of battle to cut this soliloquy in a performance. Its difficulty—serious, no doubt—is lessened if we see it as part of the entire, violent rhythm that sweeps this act after Mercutio's death. That is how it was played on the Elizabethan stage, without any interruptions, lighting effects, or set changes after every scene. The flow of the play was continuous.

IX. BLOODSTAINED FREEDOM

176 Cold judgment. Only Brecht asked for the latter, and that is why the author of this book states outright that he disagrees with Brecht's heretical view, which not even he himself observed in actual performance.

182 "Ridiculous." George Steiner, *The Death of Tragedy* (New York: Hill & Wang, 1963), p. 85.

183 "Liking for the theatre." Steiner, p. 76.

184 Its blood. I believe in the mystery of Tragedy—in the psychic sense—which is also the religious meaning of the term. Holy Communion is a tragic initiation: it does not allow substitution or "interpretation," that is, an intermediary or third person, between the lips and the flaming chalice.

184   "That of Athens." Steiner, p. 76.

184   Meet them. The French have already started wondering
      about Racine's value across time. See in *Le Monde*, October
      11, 1968, a review by B. Poirot-Delpech of a performance of
      Athalie: "These combined virtues do not overcome the
      bewilderment into which every performance sinks today."

Acknowledgments

The translator of *Homage to the Tragic Muse* is grateful to Ms. Julia Budenz, Ms. Mollie Boring, and Ms. Irene Sigalos-Rickabaugh for their valuable assistance; to his professors at Tufts University, Kalman Burnim, Sylvan Barnet, Peter Arnott, Eric Forsythe, and John Larker, for their constructive criticism and encouragement; to Professor Lowell Edmunds for his critical evaluation of the manuscript, to Cedric and Anne Whitman for their love and enthusiasm for his work; to Mr. Angelos Terzakis for answering many difficult questions; to Mr. Jeffrey Smith, Mr. Jonathan Galassi, and Ms. Randall Warner for their loving care and tireless efforts to shape and bring this book into the light.